THE COMPLETE POSTPARTUM HANDBOOK

EXTENSIVE ROADMAP TO SEAMLESS RECOVERY, MASTER NEW BABY CARE, WARD OFF NEW MOM ANXIETY AND DEPRESSION TO MANAGE THE FOURTH TRIMESTER WITH EASE

EVELYN PATRICK

8TH WONDER PUBLISHING LLC

INTRODUCTION

The early days of motherhood are filled with a mix of emotions. Imagine you've just brought your baby home. You're excited, overwhelmed, and maybe even feeling a little unsure. The house is filled with the soft cries of a newborn and the echoes of well-meaning advice from everyone around you. You're trying to keep up with diaper changes, feeding schedules, and figuring out if that sound your baby just made is normal or a cry for help. You're not alone in feeling like this.

This book is here to guide you through these moments. It's crafted to be a supportive companion as you navigate the complexities of the fourth trimester. My aim is to educate, inspire, and empower you with the information you need to find your own path in this new phase of life.

I organized this book to cover key areas that new mothers often find challenging. We'll start with physical recovery, addressing both C-section and vaginal delivery. We'll explore mental health, touching on postpartum depression and anxiety. You'll find guidance on new baby care, from breastfeeding (and what to do if that doesn't work out) to sleep training. We'll also examine relationship dynamics and how they can shift with a new baby at home. I've designed each chapter to offer insights and strategies tailored to all these topics.

I wrote this book because I've seen firsthand the struggles new mothers face. My journey into motherhood opened my eyes to the gaps in support and information available. My own experience, along with countless conversations with other mothers, drove me to write this. I have a passion for helping new moms feel confident and supported. I have poured this passion into every page, aiming to provide advice that is both evidence-based and practical.

What sets this book apart is its holistic approach. We comprehensively examine postpartum issues, considering a wide range of family dynamics. I've included relatable real-life examples to illustrate the challenges and triumphs of others who have been where you are now.

I want you to know that you are not alone. It's normal to feel uncertain and overwhelmed. This book is here to reassure you and offer guidance. It will be like having a conversation with a friend who understands and supports you. Together, we'll explore strategies, insights, and exercises to help you manage the postpartum period with ease.

You will find clear, actionable advice throughout the book. I invite you to actively engage with the content, try the exercises and strategies, and tailor them to your life and needs. This journey is yours, and this book will help you make it successful.

As we embark on the fourth trimester together, I want to leave you an inspirational note. You have the strength and courage to take on this new chapter of your life. With the right tools and support, you can face all the new challenges of this phase with confidence and grace. Welcome to motherhood, where you are supported, understood, and never alone.

NAVIGATING THE FOURTH TRIMESTER

You've just returned from the hospital, clutching your newborn close, unsure of what lies ahead. The whirlwind of emotions you're feeling is echoed in the stories of countless new mothers. This time, often called the fourth trimester, is a vital adjustment period. Unlike the first three trimesters, marked by anticipation and preparation, the fourth trimester is a time of transition and adaptation for you and your newborn. It's a period where the physical and emotional changes are as profound as they are varied. The concept of the fourth trimester suggests that babies are not quite ready for the world when they're born. They need an extra few months of a womb-like environment to adjust to life outside. For you, this means that your body and emotions are also in flux, adjusting to the monumental shift that comes with being a parent.

Understanding the Fourth Trimester: What to Expect

The fourth trimester, which spans roughly the first 12 weeks postpartum, is an extension of pregnancy. During this time, your baby is acclimating to the world, and you are learning to respond to their needs while also attending to your recovery. This phase demands patience and understanding. It will feel like a never-ending list of things to do. Your baby relies on you for comfort, warmth, and nutrition, and these needs can feel overwhelming. Yet, this bonding time is crucial. You'll be performing a lot of skin-to-skin contact and gentle rocking to help soothe your baby, strengthen your connection, and reinforce your baby's sense of security.

After childbirth, your body begins the healing process immediately. The uterus, which has grown to accommodate your baby, starts contracting back to its pre-pregnancy size. These contractions, often referred to as "afterpains," can be uncomfortable but are a sign that your body is healing. You may also experience lochia, a discharge that gradually decreases over the next few weeks. If you had a vaginal delivery, soreness is common, especially if there were tears. And for those who had a C-section, the focus will be on caring for the incision site. You also have to manage the daily challenge of sleep deprivation. Night feedings and diaper changes disrupt sleep, affecting your mood and energy levels. What else is on the list? Oh yeah, hormonal changes also play a significant role, influencing everything from mood swings to changes in weight and body shape. "Yippie!" I say that with sarcasm. This trimester can be a lot, but like all mamas, you will get through this!

Recovery doesn't follow a strict timeline, but understanding general milestones can help set your expectations. During the first six weeks, recovery is most intense. Your body needs rest and care, and it's essential to listen to its signals. By the end of this period, many mothers have a follow-up appointment with their healthcare provider to assess healing and discuss any concerns. Returning to a semblance of normalcy is gradual. Each woman's recovery varies based on a multitude of factors, including pre-birth health, delivery type, and support systems. It's crucial to be patient with yourself and recognize that everyone heals at their own pace.

Emotionally, the fourth trimester is a rollercoaster. The joy of having your baby in your arms can be tempered by anxiety and fatigue. Fluctuating hormones add to the complexity, sometimes leading to what is known as the "baby blues." These emotions are normal, but it's crucial to differentiate between temporary blues and postpartum depression, which affects many women and requires professional support. Acknowledging these feelings is the first step in managing them. Seeking help and talking about your experiences can provide relief and clarity.

Setting realistic expectations during this time is key. Motherhood is a balance of caring for your baby and maintaining your own well-being. Prioritize self-care by integrating small moments of rest and relaxation into your day. Accept help from family and friends, and do not hesitate to delegate tasks. Self-compassion is essential. Allow yourself to make mistakes and learn from them, knowing that each challenge you face is part of the journey.

Emotional Rollercoaster: Managing Postpartum Emotions

Motherhood brings many emotions. One moment, you're gazing at your baby, filled with joy, and the next, you're overwhelmed by exhaustion and anxiety. These emotional ups and downs are a natural part of the postpartum period. Remember, these feelings are normal and shared by mothers everywhere.

To maneuver through this emotional terrain, this book will highlight practical, evidence-based strategies to offer relief. For example, deep breathing exercises are a simple yet effective tool for reducing stress. Try taking a few minutes each day to focus on your breath, drawing in a deep breath through your nose, holding it for a moment, and then exhaling slowly through your mouth. This practice can help calm your mind and body, creating a momentary pause in the midst of chaos. Mindfulness and meditation practices can also serve as powerful allies. Consider setting aside a short period each day to practice mindfulness, allowing yourself to be fully present in the moment without judgment. This can help ground you and provide a sense of clarity through any emotional turbulence you might be experiencing. We will dive a little deeper into these practices in the upcoming chapters.

Recognizing and addressing postpartum depression and anxiety is crucial. The early indicators of depression, such as persistent sadness, lack of interest in activities, or feelings of hopelessness, should not be ignored. Open communication forms the backbone of emotional well-being. Sharing your feelings with your partner can foster understanding and create a supportive environment at home. It's important to express not just the joys but also the challenges you're facing.

It's also vital to understand that seeking professional help is a sign of strength, not weakness. Engaging with your healthcare provider can lead to effective interventions, whether through therapy, medication, or support groups. Postpartum Support International (PSI) is a valuable resource, offering helplines and information for those in need of assistance. Remember, you are not alone in this, and reaching out for help can make a significant difference.

In this phase, accepting the ebb and flow of emotions is part of embracing motherhood. It's okay to experience a spectrum of feelings, from elation to worry. Prioritizing your mental health through communication and practical strategies can create a more balanced and nurturing environment for both you and your baby. As you ride this emotional rollercoaster, remember that each day brings new opportunities for growth and connection.

I Remember feeling extreme anger and annoyance with my spouse during the first few weeks of postpartum, and the more everyone negated my feelings to just baby blues, the angrier I got. I wasn't sad or "blue"; I was 100% aware of my feelings. I knew it wasn't true baby blues because I was in bliss with my son, but I felt intense anger at every little wrong move my spouse made. I quickly realized the surge of hormones bouncing around in me may be the true culprit to my rage. We opted to seek couples counseling, and it made a world of difference. It was nice to have someone validate my feelings and give us strategies to handle each other with grace. Oddly, my husband was going through his own set of mental health issues with the pressures of new fatherhood brewing, so we ended up killing two birds with one stone. I wish the stigma around therapy didn't exist because it was essential to our survival during that period.

Building Your Support Network: Finding Your Tribe

The early weeks of motherhood can feel as if you're trying to juggle countless tasks while blindfolded. The sheer volume of responsibilities can be daunting. This is where a strong support network becomes invaluable. It provides not just practical assistance but emotional solace, as well. Family and friends can be your lifeline during this period. They offer a shoulder to lean on when your spirits are low and lend a hand with baby care when you need a moment to breathe. Emotional support from loved ones can alleviate the feelings of isolation that often accompany postpartum life. Practical help, such as someone cooking a meal or watching the baby while you nap, can significantly ease the burden. These acts of kindness can transform your experience, making chaos more manageable. We will discuss this in more detail in upcoming chapters.

I was lucky enough to have my mother, best friend, and cousin close by to help when my spouse and I were at our wits' end. It was a blessing to have the extra physical support. But even if you don't have easy access to a support system, many options exist. The possibilities are endless, from sitters to daycare programs or foreign exchange live-in nannies. You just have to think outside the box a little.

Emotional support is a little easier to come by than physical support. Start by considering who in your circle can be a part of your support system. Joining a new mom group is an excellent way to connect with others who understand what you're going through. These groups can be found in community centers, hospitals, or online.

They offer a platform to share experiences, exchange tips, and create bonds with those in similar situations. Online communities, such as forums or social media groups, can be just as supportive. They provide a sense of belonging and offer a space to voice concerns or celebrate milestones, day or night. Remember, it's not just about seeking support but also reciprocating it.

Asking for help might feel uncomfortable at first, but it's crucial. Recognizing that you can't do everything alone is a sign of strength. Start by crafting a postpartum support plan. This plan should outline who can assist with specific tasks, from grocery shopping to babysitting. Delegating household chores can free up precious time for you to focus on your recovery and your baby. It's about creating a balance that works for you and your family. Letting go of the need to control every detail and trusting others to step in can be liberating. I made the simple change of just having my groceries delivered, and though I had to let go of the control of produce selection, I am 100% happier knowing I've saved myself an extra hour or two.

There are times when professional support services are necessary and beneficial. Lactation consultants can provide invaluable assistance with breastfeeding challenges, offering guidance and encouragement. Postpartum doulas are another resource, offering expertise in baby care while providing you with the opportunity to rest and recuperate. These professionals bring a wealth of knowledge and experience that can ease the transition into parenthood. They are trained to support, educate, and empower you, helping you gain confidence in your new role. Whether it's learning how to latch properly or simply needing reassurance, don't hesitate to reach out to these resources.

Finding your tribe, whether through family, friends, or professional support, is about building a network that uplifts and assists you. It's about surrounding yourself with those who understand and respect your needs during this transformative time.

Balancing New Identities: Motherhood and Self

Motherhood brings with it an identity shift that can feel both exhilarating and challenging. As you step into this new role, you might find yourself reflecting on who you were before your baby arrived and contemplating how this fits with who you are becoming. This identity transformation is complex. It requires reconciling the person you were with the mother you are now. It's normal to feel pulled in different directions as you navigate the expectations of motherhood while trying to hold onto the essence of your pre-motherhood self. This intricate dance between past and present can feel like a balancing act on a tightrope, where each step requires careful thought and adjustment.

To maintain a sense of self amid the responsibilities of new motherhood, it's crucial to be proactive. Start by setting personal goals that align with your values and aspirations. These goals don't have to be monumental; they can be simple and achievable, like reading a book each month or setting aside time for a hobby you love. Prioritizing hobbies and interests is vital. These activities remind you of your individuality and provide a creative outlet separate from the demands of parenting. Whether it's painting, gardening, or writing, engaging in something that brings you joy can be a refreshing escape from daily routines.

Self-reflection is a powerful tool in this process. It allows you to acknowledge and accept the changes in your identity with grace. Consider journaling as a way to explore your thoughts and feelings. Reflect on questions like, "What aspects of my identity do I want to nurture?" or "How can I integrate my passions into my daily life?" These prompts can lead to insights that help you embrace change as a form of growth rather than loss. Embracing change is not about discarding your past self but rather weaving together the different threads of your identity into a vibrant tapestry of who you are now.

With all the vast responsibilities, self-care cannot be overlooked. Dedicating time to yourself is not indulgent; it is necessary for your mental and emotional well-being. Create a self-care schedule that includes activities that recharge you, even if it's just a few minutes each day. Mindful relaxation techniques, such as deep breathing or progressive muscle relaxation, can help alleviate stress and bring a sense of calm. Consider setting aside specific times for these practices, perhaps when your baby naps or in the quiet moments of the evening. By prioritizing self-care, you are investing in your own health and happiness, which in turn benefits your family.

As you approach the identity shift that accompanies motherhood, remember that it's a dynamic process. It's about finding harmony between old and new, blending your past experiences with the present demands. This integration allows you to step confidently into your role as a mother while honoring the person you have always been. Rather than seeing this as a loss of identity, view it as an expansion, a way to enrich your life with new dimensions and perspectives.

Debunking Postpartum Myths: Realistic Expectations

As you step into motherhood, you might find yourself surrounded by a myriad of myths and misconceptions that can cloud your expectations. One of the most persistent myths is that of the "perfect" mother. This idea suggests that you should know instinctively how to care for your baby without any mistakes. Society often portrays this image of a mother who is always calm, always capable, and never falters. But the truth is perfection is unattainable and unrealistic. Every mother has her moments of doubt and uncertainty. It's essential to recognize that making mistakes does not diminish your capability or love as a mother. Instead, these experiences provide opportunities for growth and learning.

Another common misconception is the expectation of immediate bonding with your baby. While some mothers feel an instant connection, others find that this bond develops gradually. Both experiences are entirely normal. The pressure to feel an immediate attachment can lead to unnecessary stress and self-doubt. It's essential to allow yourself the grace to bond with your baby in your own time without comparing your experience to others. Remember, each relationship is unique and unfolds differently. The love and bond you share will deepen each day as you and your baby learn and grow together.

To counter these myths, you must arm yourself with evidence-based information. Postpartum recovery is not a race. It doesn't follow a strict timeline, and each mother's experience is unique. While some may feel physically and emotionally stable within a few weeks, others may take longer. This variation is normal and influenced by numerous factors, including your health before pregnancy and the nature of your delivery. Embrace the diversity of postpartum experiences and understand there is no one-size-fits-all approach. Acknowledging this will allow you to set realistic expectations for yourself and your recovery.

Setting achievable goals can help you navigate this period with confidence. Focus on small, manageable targets rather than overwhelming yourself with unrealistic expectations. Whether it's getting some rest, spending quality time with your baby, or simply taking a shower, these small victories add up. Cultivating a flexible mindset allows you to adapt to the ever-changing demands of motherhood. Flexibility enables you to respond to unexpected challenges with resilience and creativity. It also helps in letting go of rigid plans when things don't go as expected, which they often won't.

Practicing self-compassion is another crucial element in maintaining your well-being. Many mothers hold themselves to impossibly high standards, believing they must do everything perfectly. But the truth is, you're human, and it's okay to stumble. By practicing self-forgiveness, you can release the burden of guilt and move forward with kindness towards yourself. Letting go of perfectionism is liberating. It allows you to embrace the messiness of motherhood with a sense of humor and grace. By accepting that imperfection is part of the process, you can focus on what truly matters: the love and connection you share with your baby.

Remember, myths and misconceptions can create unnecessary pressure. Setting realistic expectations and embracing self-compassion will foster a nurturing environment for you and your baby. This period is about learning and growing, not about measuring up to an unattainable ideal. Trust your instincts, seek support when needed, and know your unique path is valid and worthy. With understanding and empathy, you can confidently face the challenges ahead, knowing you are doing your best for yourself and your family.

PHYSICAL RECOVERY AND PELVIC HEALTH

You're lying in bed, the soft morning light filtering through the curtains, your newborn nestled beside you, breathing softly. You feel a sense of wonder mixed with an overwhelming fatigue. The exertion your body has undertaken to bring life into the world is nothing short of miraculous, yet now it demands care and attention as it begins to heal. Postpartum recovery is a process that unfolds over time, with each day bringing you closer to feeling like yourself again. Understanding this timeline and what to expect can help ease the challenges and uncertainties of the coming weeks.

Healing After Vaginal Delivery: Steps to Recovery

In the initial days following a vaginal delivery, your body begins a remarkable transformation. The most significant physical changes mark the first few weeks as your body works to heal and adapt. Uterine involution, the process where your uterus shrinks back to its pre-pregnancy size, is a key aspect of this recovery. You might experience afterpains similar to mild contractions, especially during breastfeeding, as breastfeeding stimulates the release of oxytocin, which aids in this process of the uterus contracting back to size as well as reducing postpartum bleeding. Oxytocin also has a natural pain-relieving effect. Skin-to-skin contact with your baby can also help release oxytocin if you have chosen not to breastfeed or are unable to.

During vaginal childbirth, the perineum stretches to allow the baby to pass, but this can sometimes result in perineal tears, which may be corrected with stitches or a surgical incision, episiotomy, which is no longer common. The perineum, which is the area of tissue between the vaginal opening and anus, can have some discomfort after delivery. This discomfort can be more extreme for some but is manageable. I remember being paranoid about the whole tearing process. I just kept thinking, what if my vagina completely rips? How on earth will I go to the bathroom, or wipe, for that matter? But honestly, with everything going on during the birthing process, it's barely a noticeable experience. Swelling, tenderness, and soreness in the perineal area can make sitting and moving around uncomfortable. Granted, everyone has a different tolerance for pain, but I felt like the discomfort was minimal.

So let me reassure you: the female body is extraordinary, and tearing is a common part of the process; things will almost miraculously return to the way they were. Your doctor will carefully repair the tear using dissolvable stitches. Even with my in-depth mirror examination, I could never find them. After each trip to the bathroom, I simply flushed the area with a peri-bottle, which was very soothing. Afterward, I recommend gently patting the area dry instead of wiping. It's the same process for bowel movements, but remember to wipe gently from behind to avoid contamination. Stool Softeners can make bowel movements easier because it's important not to strain or put more stress on the area than necessary. I used Tucks' witch hazel pads to aid healing and comfort. For an extra hack, you can chill the Tucks' pads.

Postpartum bleeding, known as lochia, is another normal part of recovery and can last up to six weeks. It's important to note that lochia will still occur after a c-section. It starts as a heavy, bright red flow and gradually fades to pink or brown before stopping. Managing these symptoms is crucial to supporting your healing. I preferred to wear incontinence disposable underwear like Depends during this time. They provided ease of use and handled excess bleeding much better than pads. For perineal discomfort, ice packs or cold compresses can help reduce swelling and numb the area, providing relief. Sitz baths, where you soak your perineal area in warm water, can promote healing and offer soothing comfort. These simple yet effective home remedies can be incorporated into your daily routine, making a significant difference in your comfort and recovery.

Listening to your body and understanding when to seek medical advice is essential. While some discomfort and bleeding are normal, some signs should prompt you to contact your healthcare provider. Heavy bleeding that soaks a pad within an hour, large blood clots, or a foul-smelling discharge can signal a problem. Similarly, if you notice any signs of infection, such as fever, increased pain, or redness and swelling around your stitches, contact your healthcare provider promptly. These symptoms may indicate complications that require medical intervention. Your health and well-being are a priority, and addressing concerns early on can prevent further issues.

 In these early days, rest is paramount. Allow yourself to take things slow, focusing on small, achievable tasks. Long-term recovery varies, but many women start feeling more like themselves within six to eight weeks postpartum. However, remember that everybody is different, and your recovery timeline may differ from others.

Reflection Section: Tracking Your Recovery

Keeping a journal of your recovery can be a helpful tool. Note any symptoms you experience, their duration, and any remedies you find effective. This practice not only helps you track your progress but also provides valuable information for discussions with your healthcare provider. Consider including reflections on your emotional well-being, capturing moments of joy and any challenges you face. These reflections can serve as a beautiful reminder of your strength during this transformative time.

As you begin to heal after vaginal delivery, remember that patience is your ally. Your body has accomplished something extraordinary and deserves the time and care required to recover fully. Each step you take, whether it's a gentle walk around the block or a moment of rest with your baby in your arms, brings you closer to renewed strength and vitality.

C-Section Recovery: Navigating the Healing Process

As you transition into the postpartum phase following a C-section, it's crucial to understand the path your body will take to recover. The experience can be quite different from vaginal delivery, as a C-section is major abdominal surgery. Most women typically leave the hospital within one to two days, but the healing process continues for several weeks. During this period, managing the incision site is essential. You'll likely have a horizontal scar, usually below the bikini line, which may feel tender and sore. It's normal to experience pain and discomfort lasting for weeks on end.

Hospital staff will provide painkillers to help manage this discomfort, and it's essential to take these as directed to ensure adequate pain relief. Avoid aspirin, as it can increase bleeding risks. If you are breastfeeding, it's important to know that most pain medications will pass into breast milk but in tiny amounts that are unlikely to harm the baby. They can also decrease your milk supply. Potential effects on the baby could include lethargy, feeding difficulties, and, in rare cases, respiratory issues. You should monitor your baby closely or discuss your concerns with your doctor before taking any pain medications. Use prescribed pain medications responsibly, following your healthcare provider's guidance. Alternative pain relief techniques like deep breathing exercises and relaxation practices should also be explored. These methods can complement medications and provide holistic relief.

Caring for your surgical scar is a significant aspect of recovery. Proper care can promote healing and minimize scarring. Once the dressing is removed after at least 24 hours, gently cleanse the area with mild soap and water. You might consider using scar creams or ointments, which can aid in reducing scar visibility over time. Once your healthcare provider approves, gentle massage techniques can also be helpful. They increase circulation and promote collagen production, which supports the healing process. Remember to be gentle and patient with your body during this time. It's undergoing substantial recovery, and nurturing it with care and attention is key.

It's also important to be aware of potential complications. Recognizing early signs and seeking timely medical advice can prevent serious issues. If you notice any symptoms of infection, such as redness, swelling, increased pain, or discharge at the incision site, contact your healthcare provider immediately. Other warning signs include fever, heavy bleeding, or foul smells around your incision. These symptoms could indicate an infection or other complications that require medical intervention. Monitor yourself for signs of deep vein thrombosis, like sudden leg pain or swelling. If you suspect any of these issues, don't hesitate to seek help. Your health and safety are paramount, and addressing concerns promptly ensures a smoother recovery.

As you start to regain your strength, you'll be encouraged to move around gently to facilitate recovery. Walking is highly beneficial. It promotes circulation, boosts mood, and helps prevent complications such as blood clots. However, it's vital to avoid heavy lifting and intense physical activity until your healthcare provider gives the go-ahead.

The importance of mobility cannot be overstated. Start with short walks around your home, gradually increasing the distance as you feel more comfortable. Balance is essential, so listen to your body's signals and avoid pushing yourself too hard. Over-exertion can hinder recovery and lead to complications.

Patience and self-compassion are your greatest allies in navigating C-section recovery. Embrace the support of loved ones and healthcare professionals as you heal. Celebrate small milestones and allow yourself the grace to recover at your own pace. Your body has accomplished an incredible task, so allow it to move forward gently.

Navigating Post-Epidural Symptoms

It's natural to feel concerned if you're experiencing symptoms after having an epidural, but it's important to know that most post-epidural side effects are temporary and manageable. Mild discomfort at the injection site, such as tenderness or bruising, is common and typically resolves within a few days. Some women may also experience a headache known as a post-dural puncture headache, which can occur if a small amount of spinal fluid is affected during the procedure. While this type of headache can feel intense, it usually improves with rest, hydration, and sometimes a simple procedure called a blood patch. Remember, these symptoms don't mean something has gone wrong; they're simply part of the body's recovery process after childbirth and an epidural.

If you're worried about lingering symptoms like back pain or tingling, knowing that these sensations are usually temporary and not uncommon is helpful. The back pain often relates to the physical strain of labor or postpartum adjustments rather than the epidural itself. However, if you feel unsure or symptoms persist, reaching out to your healthcare provider for reassurance or evaluation is always a good step. I felt a strange numbness and tingling sensation along the inside of my thigh right after birth, and my doctor referred me to a neurologist who reassured me that sometimes nerves take a little longer to recover. He said to give it six more weeks, and he was right! Many mothers who experience side effects after an epidural go on to recover fully without lasting issues. Take comfort in knowing that your body is incredibly resilient, and with time and proper care, it will continue to heal and adjust after the monumental experience of childbirth.

Postpartum Glow and Growth: Understanding Skin, Hair, and Nail Changes

As you adjust to life postpartum, you may notice unexpected changes in your skin, hair, and nails; this is just another reminder that your body is dynamic during this phase. Skin changes are common, ranging from lingering pigmentation like melasma to the gradual fading of stretch marks. While melasma, often called the "mask of pregnancy," may take time to lighten, consistent use of sunscreen and gentle skincare can help. Stretch marks, too, evolve, often becoming less prominent as the months pass. It's important to remember that these marks and changes are a testament to your body's incredible journey and ability to adapt.

Hair and nail changes may also take center stage in the months after birth. Postpartum hair loss, caused by hormonal shifts, can feel alarming as more strands than usual shed. Rest assured, this is temporary, and hair growth often resumes within a few months. Similarly, your nails may feel more brittle or prone to breaking, another sign of your body rebalancing. Focusing on nourishing your body with vitamins, minerals, and hydration can support healthy regrowth for both hair and nails. While temporary, these changes remind you of the transformation your body has undergone. With care and time, your natural balance will return.

Breast Tissue Changes

In the early days of breastfeeding, your breasts undergo significant changes as they adapt to milk production. You may experience engorgement, a condition where your breasts feel overly full, firm, and tender; this typically occurs when your milk supply begins to regulate, often within the first few weeks postpartum. While it can be uncomfortable, applying warm compresses before feeding and cool compresses afterward can help relieve the swelling. A proper breastfeeding schedule and ensuring your baby has a good latch are crucial to managing engorgement. Understanding that this phase is temporary can provide reassurance as you adjust to the feeding rhythms.

However, some mothers may face challenges like mastitis, an inflammation of the breast tissue that can lead to pain, redness, and even flu-like symptoms such as fever and chills. Mastitis often results from clogged milk ducts or incomplete breast emptying during feeds. Prompt attention is essential; continuing to breastfeed or pump regularly, along with gentle massage, can help clear blockages. In more severe cases, consulting a healthcare provider for antibiotics or additional support may be necessary. Beyond these immediate concerns, long-term breast shape and size changes may also occur. Embracing these changes and focusing on strategies to ensure your comfort can empower you to approach breastfeeding with confidence.

Pelvic Floor Health: Exercises and Insights

As you adjust to life as a new mother, you should focus on your health, and one area that deserves your attention is your pelvic floor. This group of muscles supports the bladder, uterus, and bowel and is crucial in continence and core stability. Childbirth can weaken these muscles. Maintaining pelvic floor strength is vital for preventing these problems and ensuring long-term pelvic health. Imagine your pelvic floor as a supportive hammock, holding everything in place. When it weakens, it can't do its job effectively, leading to discomfort and incontinence.

Strengthening your pelvic floor doesn't require expensive equipment or a gym membership. You can practice simple exercises right at home. Kegel exercises are a popular and easy way to strengthen these muscles. To perform them, sit comfortably and imagine you are trying to stop the flow of urine. Tighten the muscles, hold for a few seconds, then release. You can begin these exercises within a few days postpartum. Repeat this process several times a day, gradually increasing the duration as your strength improves. Another beneficial exercise is the pelvic tilt. Lie on your back with your knees bent and feet flat on the floor. Gently lift your pelvis upward, engaging your core muscles, and hold for a few seconds before lowering. These exercises are discreet and can be done nearly anywhere, making them easy to incorporate into your daily routine.

While self-guided exercises can be effective, sometimes professional guidance can make a significant difference. Pelvic floor therapy offers a targeted approach to recovery tailored to your specific needs. A therapist can provide a personalized plan, focusing on exercises and techniques that address your concerns. This professional support not only aids in immediate recovery but also contributes to long-term pelvic health. Many women find that working with a therapist helps them regain confidence and control more quickly.

Another common issue is pelvic organ prolapse, where the pelvic organs drop due to weakened muscles. Symptoms can include a feeling of heaviness or discomfort in the pelvic area. Addressing these symptoms early with targeted exercises and, if necessary, medical intervention can prevent them from becoming more severe.

You can strengthen and support these muscles by recognizing issues early, incorporating exercises into your routine, and seeking professional help when needed. This will prove to be very beneficial in the years to come.

Diastasis Recti: Understanding and Managing

As you gaze down at your postpartum belly, you may notice changes that go beyond stretch marks and softness. Diastasis recti is a condition that affects many new mothers and is characterized by the separation of the abdominal muscles along the midline. This occurs when the connective tissue, called the linea alba, stretches during pregnancy to accommodate your growing baby. The impact of diastasis recti extends beyond aesthetics, potentially affecting your core strength and posture. A weakened core can lead to back pain, pelvic floor dysfunction, and a feeling of instability in your movements. Understanding diastasis recti is the first step in managing its effects and reclaiming your core strength.

Identifying diastasis recti involves a simple self-assessment. Lie on your back with your knees bent and feet flat on the floor. Gently lift your head and shoulders off the ground as if you're doing a crunch. Feel along the midline of your abdomen with your fingers, starting from just below the rib cage down to the pubic bone. If you notice a gap or a soft area that feels wider than two fingers, you might have diastasis recti. While self-assessment is a helpful tool, consulting with a physical therapist can provide a more accurate diagnosis. A therapist can evaluate the severity of the separation and recommend a personalized treatment plan to aid recovery.

Recovery from diastasis recti involves specific exercises that focus on strengthening the transverse abdominis, the deepest layer of abdominal muscles. These exercises help draw the separated muscles back together, improving core stability. You can begin these exercises 2-4 weeks postpartum. Start with gentle exercises such as pelvic tilts, where you lie on your back and gently tilt your pelvis upward, engaging your core. Another effective exercise is the transverse abdominis activation, which involves drawing your belly button toward your spine while maintaining relaxed shoulders and even breathing. These exercises should be performed consistently, gradually increasing in intensity as your strength improves. It's crucial to avoid exercises that may exacerbate the condition, such as traditional crunches and planks, which can place undue stress on the abdominal muscles.

While many women can manage diastasis recti effectively with at-home exercises, there are instances where professional treatment becomes necessary. If the separation is significant or accompanied by pain or discomfort, seeking the guidance of a physical therapist is advisable. Physical therapy offers targeted exercises and techniques to support your recovery. Therapists can also provide guidance on proper posture and movement patterns to prevent further strain on your core. In severe cases where diastasis recti leads to functional impairments or is resistant to conservative treatments, surgical intervention may be considered. Abdominoplasty is a surgical procedure that can repair the separation, restoring the integrity and function of the abdominal wall. However, surgery is typically reserved for cases where other treatments have failed, and discussing all options with your healthcare provider is essential.

Understanding diastasis recti and taking proactive steps to manage it can significantly impact your postpartum recovery. By incorporating core-strengthening exercises into your routine and seeking professional support when necessary, you can improve your core strength, enhance your posture, and alleviate discomfort. Mild cases of diastasis recti can heal within 3-6 months, but moderate to severe cases may take 6-12 months. Remember, the path to recovery is personal and unique to each individual.

Safe Postpartum Fitness: Gradual and Effective Routines

As you transition into motherhood, returning to physical activity can feel like an enormous task. Your body has undergone significant changes, and you should approach your path back to fitness with care and patience. A gradual return to exercise is crucial to avoid injury and over-exertion. Your body needs time to rebuild strength and stamina; rushing this process can lead to setbacks. Think of this period as a time to reacquaint yourself with your body's new needs and capabilities. Listening to your body and recognizing its signals for rest is essential.

When creating a postpartum fitness plan, start with low-impact exercises. These activities are gentle on your joints and muscles, making them ideal for easing back into a routine. Walking is an excellent starting point; it's low impact, can be done almost anywhere, and offers an opportunity to enjoy fresh air. Swimming is another option; the buoyancy of the water supports your body, reducing strain while providing an effective workout. As you gain confidence and strength, consider incorporating flexibility and strength training. Gentle yoga and Pilates are perfect for this, as they focus on core strength, balance, and flexibility. They also offer a moment of relaxation and mindfulness, which can benefit your mental and physical health.

Professional guidance can play a pivotal role in your postpartum fitness. Working with one specializing in postpartum care can provide personalized insights and assessments. Their expertise can guide you safely through exercises, helping you avoid common pitfalls and injuries. They can also offer customized assessments of your current fitness level and set realistic goals for the months ahead. I opted to do YouTube videos geared toward my postpartum fitness level and prioritized my form and ability to do specific movements. I highly recommend Jessica Pumple's YouTube channel, Pregnancy and Postpartum TV.

Remember, the goal is not to rush the process but to enjoy it, finding joy in movement and your progress. Your postpartum fitness is unique, and honoring your body's needs is paramount. With patience, support, and a thoughtful approach, you will rebuild your strength and agility and be ready to embrace motherhood. Each step you take is a step towards physical recovery and a renewed sense of self.

By the end of this chapter, you should feel equipped with the knowledge to tackle your postpartum health and fitness with ease. Next, we'll focus on mastering new baby care, ensuring you and your little one thrive.

MASTERING NEW BABY CARE

Bringing your newborn home is a beautiful experience but can also bring uncertainty and countless questions. One of the first challenges you'll master is understanding their feeding needs and rhythms, which will set the foundation for their growth and your confidence as a parent. Newborns have tiny stomachs and digest formula or breastmilk quickly, so they need to be fed frequently.

Formula-fed babies usually eat every 3 to 4 hours, starting with 1 to 2 ounces per feeding and increasing to 2 to 3 ounces as they grow, typically by the two-week mark. Growth spurts, which often happen around 1 to 3 weeks, 6 weeks, and 3 months, may lead to even more frequent feedings. As long as your baby has 6 to 8 wet diapers a day and is gaining weight steadily, they're likely getting enough. If you're ever unsure, though, reach out to your pediatrician for guidance.

If breastfeeding, aim to feed your baby every 2 to 3 hours, which typically adds up to 8 to 12 times in 24 hours. Keep an eye out for hunger cues like rooting, sucking on their hands, or general fussiness, and let them nurse for 10 to 20 minutes on each breast or until they seem content.

The benefits of breastfeeding extend beyond the immediate, offering a lifetime of health advantages. Breast milk is a nutritional powerhouse for your baby, providing all the essential nutrients they need for growth and development. It's rich in antibodies, boosting your baby's immune system and offering protection against common illnesses. For you, breastfeeding can reduce the risk of certain cancers, like breast and ovarian, and help your body recover from pregnancy and childbirth more quickly. This natural process is a beautiful symbiosis of giving and receiving, strengthening your body and your bond with your baby.

Foundational principles of breastfeeding set the stage for success. Skin-to-skin contact is vital, fostering a connection that enhances emotional bonding and milk production. Holding your baby against your bare chest right after birth not only calms them but also encourages their instinct to nurse. Understanding the mechanics of a good latch is crucial. A successful latch ensures your baby is feeding effectively and prevents your discomfort. It's the cornerstone of breastfeeding, influencing everything from milk supply to your baby's weight gain. Recognizing when your baby is ready to feed is another important aspect. Hunger cues can include rooting, turning their head toward your breast, or making sucking motions. Responding to these cues promptly helps establish a rhythm that meets your baby's needs and supports your milk production.

Achieving a proper latch can be challenging, but with patience and practice, it becomes second nature. A good latch starts by tickling your baby's lips with your nipple, encouraging them to open their mouth wide. Aim the nipple just above their top lip and guide them to lead with their chin, ensuring their mouth covers the areola, not just the nipple. This position helps your baby get enough milk and makes breastfeeding more comfortable. Their lips should be flanged outward, resembling a fish, and their chin should press into your breast. You'll know the latch is correct if breastfeeding feels comfortable and you see your baby's cheeks rhythmically moving as they swallow. Occasionally, you might need to adjust the baby's position to achieve a better latch. Techniques like the cross-cradle or football hold can offer different angles and support, making the process easier for both of you.

The football hold, also known as the clutch hold, is a breastfeeding position where the baby is tucked under the mother's arm on the same side as the breast they are feeding from. The baby's head is being supported by the mother's hand while the body extends along the mother's side, often resting on a nursing pillow for additional support. This position is particularly beneficial for mothers who have had a C-section, as it keeps the baby away from the incision site, reducing discomfort. It's also an excellent option for mothers with larger breasts or those breastfeeding twins, as it provides easy access to both breasts without much adjustment. The football hold gives the mother a clear view of the baby's latch, making it easier to ensure proper positioning.

The cradle hold is one of the most common and traditional breast-feeding positions. In this hold, the baby's head rests in the crook of the mother's arm on the side being fed, with the baby's body lying across the mother's chest and stomach. The mother uses her other hand to guide the baby to latch or provide additional support to the baby's back. This position is comfortable for many mothers, espe-cially after establishing breastfeeding, as it requires less effort to maintain. However, it can be more challenging for newborns still learning to latch properly, as the mother's view of the latch is more obstructed than in the football hold.

Take time to observe your baby's feeding patterns. Note what posi-tions work best and how your baby responds. Use a journal to track these insights, jotting down any questions or concerns to discuss with a lactation consultant. Practicing in a calm environment can improve your confidence and comfort, making each feeding session a rewarding experience.

Navigating Breastfeeding Challenges: Common Struggles and Solutions

Breastfeeding, while deeply rewarding, can come with its own set of challenges. For many mothers, the initial days of breastfeeding may involve learning curves and unexpected difficulties. One common issue is tongue tie, a condition where the thin piece of tissue under a baby's tongue restricts its movement. This can make latching difficult, leading to discomfort for the mother and inefficient feeding for the baby. If you suspect tongue-tie, consult a pediatrician or lactation consultant. They can assess the situation and recommend interventions, such as a minor procedure to release the restriction. After the support and guidance, you and your baby will be much more comfortable breastfeeding.

Nipple discomfort or damage is another frequent concern, often caused by an improper latch or extended feeding sessions. To care for your nipples, ensure your baby is latching deeply, with their mouth covering more than just the nipple itself. Using a lanolin cream or hydrogel pads can provide relief and promote healing. Air-drying your nipples after feeding and wearing breathable, soft bras can also help reduce irritation. If the pain persists, seek help from a lactation consultant; they can observe and offer personalized advice.

Other struggles, such as low milk supply or overproduction, can also arise. If you're worried about supply, nursing on demand and ensuring proper hydration and nutrition are key. Galactagogues, such as oatmeal or fenugreek, may help boost production, though it's always best to consult a healthcare provider before trying supplements. For overproduction, expressing a small amount of milk before feeding can reduce engorgement and make latching easier for your baby. Pumping and storing excess can also be beneficial. Remember, every challenge is an opportunity to learn and adapt.

As you navigate the complexities of breastfeeding, remember that each session is a step toward mastering this essential skill. It's a dance of learning and adapting for you and your baby. With each feeding, you build a rhythm that nourishes and nurtures, creating a foundation of health and love that will support your child for years to come.

The Power of Pumping: Flexibility and Nourishment

For many new moms, breastmilk pumping offers a versatile way to provide nourishment for their babies while accommodating the demands of modern life. Pumping allows you to store breastmilk for times when you're away, giving you flexibility without compromising your baby's nutrition. It can also be a helpful tool to relieve engorgement, stimulate milk production, or share feeding responsibilities with a partner. Whether you're returning to work, need a break, or simply want the option to feed your baby on your terms, pumping can be a practical solution.

Exclusive pumping is another path many mothers choose, either out of necessity or preference. This approach involves expressing all your baby's milk needs with a pump instead of nursing directly at the breast. It can be an empowering choice for mothers who face challenges like latch issues, tongue-tie, or personal comfort. Exclusive pumping requires dedication, as it involves a regular schedule to maintain milk supply, but it also offers unique benefits. It allows you to know exactly how much milk your baby consumes and gives you a sense of control and confidence in your ability to feed.

If you decide to incorporate pumping, setting yourself up for success with the right tools and strategies is essential. Invest in a quality breast pump that meets your needs, whether a hospital-grade pump for efficiency or a portable one for convenience. I tried so many options for pumps; if I can save another mom the headache, trust me, just go for hospital grade. It gives you the best outcome for milk extraction. Another issue I had was not selecting the appropriate flange size for my nipple; most flanges come standard and tend to be much too large for those smaller nipple mamas.

Luckily, there are silicone flange inserts that come in all sizes. You can use them to customize the flanges that come with your pump to your unique nipple size. Another tip is to find a nipple cream to aid in nipple comfort while pumping. For me, I found lanolin to be great for breastfeeding but preferred more of a nipple butter for pumping.

Next, create a pumping schedule that mimics your baby's feeding patterns to maintain supply, and remember to store milk safely following proper guidelines. Also, there are many pump attachment options that can deliver milk straight into storage bags instead of bottles. It's one less step, saves on freezer space, and can help you store every single drop. I used and loved Kiinde twist pouches. Pumping, whether exclusively or alongside nursing, is a labor of love that nourishes your baby. Every ounce you provide is a testament to your care and dedication.

It's important to note that you can freeze breast milk to preserve its nutrients and ensure a safe feeding option for your baby later. However, how long it stays safe and effective depends on the type of freezer you use. Here are the guidelines for freezing breast milk:

Storage Times for Frozen Breast Milk

1 Freezer Inside a Refrigerator (Top or Side Compartment): Breast milk can be stored for **3-6 months**. Ensure the freezer maintains a consistent temperature of 0°F (-18°C) or colder.

2 Stand-Alone Freezer (Separate from the Refrigerator): Milk stored in a deep freezer or chest freezer, which maintains a constant temperature of -4°F (-20°C), can last **up to 12 months**. However, for optimal quality, I recommend using it within 6 months.

Tips for Freezing and Storing Breast Milk

• **Use Proper Containers**: Store milk in BPA-free breast milk storage bags or hard plastic/glass containers with airtight lids. Leave some space at the top to allow for expansion during freezing.

• **Label Clearly**: Write the date of expression on each container so you can use the oldest milk first.

• **Avoid Storing Milk in Door Compartments**. Keep it in the back of the freezer, where the temperature is most consistent.

• **Thawing and Using Frozen Milk**: Thaw breast milk in the refrigerator overnight or by placing it in warm water. Once thawed, use within 24 hours and never refreeze.

By following these guidelines, you can safely provide your baby with the benefits of breast milk, even after freezing.

Formula Feeding: Understanding Your Options

It's the middle of the night; your baby is stirring and fussing in your arms. You walk to the kitchen, where you quickly prepare a bottle, feeling grateful for the flexibility this option provides. Bottle feeding is a valid and beneficial choice for many families, offering a sense of freedom and convenience that breastfeeding may not always allow. With bottle feeding, you can share the responsibility of feeding with your partner or other caregivers, allowing for much-needed rest and recovery. It also offers the ability to adhere to a flexible schedule, making it easier to manage other responsibilities or return to work. This shared experience can foster bonding between your baby and other family members, enriching their relationships and providing you with valuable support.

When considering formula feeding, it's easy to get bogged down by all the different types of formulas available. But let's discuss some of the main choices. Cow's milk-based formulas are the most common, designed to resemble breast milk in nutrient composition. They offer a balanced mix of carbohydrates, fats, and proteins that support your baby's growth. Goat's milk-based formulas can be a suitable alternative for babies with cow's milk sensitivities, offering similar nutritional benefits with a different protein structure. For lactose-free options, soy-based formulas provide a plant-based alternative that can ease digestive issues in some infants. Hypoallergenic formulas are specially designed for babies with allergies, using proteins that are broken down into smaller parts, making them easier to digest. Each type has pros and cons, and the choice often depends on your baby's needs and dietary restrictions.

Every baby is unique, and their nutritional needs can vary. Consulting your pediatrician is crucial when selecting a formula, especially if your baby shows signs of allergies, digestive issues, or feeding challenges.

Common concerns and myths about formula feeding can sometimes overshadow its benefits. Some worry about formula safety, but rest assured, all infant formulas in the U.S. meet strict FDA standards for nutrition and safety. Misconceptions about nutritional content can lead to guilt or doubt. But all formulas are designed to provide your baby with a complete and balanced diet. Embracing positive self-talk and affirming your feeding choices can alleviate guilt and reinforce confidence in your decision to formula feed.

Like breast milk, formula does not require additional water for hydration, as it already contains the necessary water amounts once mixed. Please note you should not give plain water until your baby is at least six months old and has started solid foods. Newborns have specific nutritional and hydration needs, and their tiny bodies are not yet equipped to handle plain water.

Preparing and storing baby formula correctly is crucial to maintaining its safety and nutritional quality. Always follow the instructions on the formula packaging for the correct water-to-powder ratio, ensuring your baby receives the nutrients they need without dilution or concentration errors. Keep prepared bottles in the refrigerator and use them within 24 hours. Avoid using the microwave to warm the formula; it can create uneven heating and hot spots. Instead, you should warm bottles by placing them in a bowl of warm water or using a bottle warmer. After each feeding, discard any leftover formula to prevent bacterial growth. Thoroughly clean and sanitize bottles, nipples, and any feeding equipment, ensuring a safe feeding experience every time.

Choosing the right bottle and nipple can significantly impact your bottle-feeding experience. Look for bottles with features that mimic breastfeeding to ease transitions, such as slow-flow nipples that allow your baby to feed at their own pace. Bonding during bottle feeding is just as crucial as during breastfeeding, and holding your baby close while maintaining eye contact can nurture this connection. If you're supplementing or transitioning from breastfeeding to formula, introduce the bottle gradually, allowing your baby time to adjust to the new experience. Alternate between breast and bottle to maintain your milk supply and help your baby adapt to both feeding methods.

Skin-to-Skin Contact: The Science of Bonding

There you are, holding your newborn close, feeling the warmth of their skin against yours. These moments of skin-to-skin contact are more than just comforting; they are foundational to your baby's development and your relationship. This practice, often called "kangaroo care," is essential in promoting an emotional connection between you and your baby. Holding your baby directly on your bare chest creates a soothing environment that calms them, reduces crying, and helps regulate their heart rate and temperature. This closeness fosters a sense of security and trust, laying the groundwork for a strong emotional bond. As your baby nestles against you, they begin to recognize your scent, the rhythm of your heartbeat, and the warmth of your skin, all of which provide a sense of safety and comfort.

Find a quiet, comfortable spot, and gently place your baby on your chest, covering them with a soft blanket to keep them warm. Use these times to relax and connect, free from distractions. Whether after a bath or before bedtime, these moments of closeness can become cherished rituals that strengthen your bond.

The impact of skin-to-skin contact extends beyond bonding; as stated before, it plays a significant role in breastfeeding success. When your baby rests against your skin, this contact stimulates the release of hormones that promote milk production, enhancing breastfeeding initiation. The sense of security provided by skin-to-skin contact helps your baby latch more effectively, increasing the chances of successful breastfeeding. This connection also aids in recognizing your baby's natural feeding cues, such as rooting or sucking motions, allowing you to respond promptly to their needs. The more frequently you engage in skin-to-skin, the more attuned you become to your baby's signals, creating a harmonious feeding relationship.

For premature infants, skin-to-skin contact offers even greater benefits. In the Neonatal Intensive Care Unit (NICU), where the environment can feel overwhelming, skin-to-skin contact provides a sanctuary of calm and connection. It helps stabilize premature babies' heart rates, improves their oxygen levels, and supports weight gain. For NICU families, kangaroo care becomes a vital part of their caregiving routine, empowering parents to take an active role in their baby's care. It transforms a challenging experience into one filled with hope and healing. The following will guide you through this process:

How Long Should Skin-to-Skin Last?

• Immediately After Birth:

○ At least **1 hour** of uninterrupted skin-to-skin contact. This "golden hour" promotes bonding, stabilizes the baby's temperature, and supports breastfeeding initiation.

• Daily Practice:

○ **30 minutes to 1 hour per session**, several times a day, is ideal in the early weeks. This can be adjusted based on you and your baby's needs.

How Often Should Skin-to-Skin Be Done?

• **In the First Few Weeks**:

○ Skin-to-skin contact is especially beneficial in the first **1-3 months postpartum** while the baby adjusts to life outside the womb. Daily sessions are encouraged, particularly during feeding or to soothe the baby.

• **As Needed Beyond the Newborn Stage**:

○ While frequent sessions are most impactful in the early weeks, continuing skin-to-skin as the baby grows can still offer comfort, promote bonding, and support breastfeeding.

When to Do Skin-to-Skin

• **Right After Birth**:

○ Place the baby on the mother's bare chest, ideally within minutes of birth.

• **During Feedings**:

○ Both breastfeeding and bottle-feeding can incorporate skin-to-skin to strengthen the bond and encourage milk production.

• **When Calming the Baby**:

○ Skin-to-skin can soothe a fussy baby, reduce stress, and improve sleep.

• **For Kangaroo Care (Preemies)**:

○ Preterm babies benefit significantly from frequent skin-to-skin sessions, which sometimes last **1-2 hours and occur** multiple times a day.

Benefits of Skin-to-Skin for Mothers and Babies

• **For the Baby**:

o Regulates temperature, heart rate, and breathing.

o Reduces crying and stress.

o Promotes breastfeeding success.

• **For the Mother**:

o Increases oxytocin levels, promoting bonding and milk production.

o Helps with postpartum healing and emotional well-being.

o Reduces the risk of postpartum depression.

Practical Tips

• **Set a Routine**: Incorporate skin-to-skin into feeding or naptime routines.

• **Be Comfortable**: Wear a button-down shirt or skin-to-skin wrap for convenience.

• **Partners Can Participate**: Fathers or other caregivers can also engage in skin-to-skin to bond with the baby.

The Gentle Art of Bathing Your Newborn

Bathing your newborn is a tender and special ritual; it's a moment to connect with your baby while gently caring for their delicate skin. In those early weeks, sponge baths are often the best approach until your baby's umbilical cord stump falls off. You can carefully clean their face, hands, and diaper area using warm, not hot water and a soft washcloth. Also, focus on the neck and folds where milk and sweat accumulate. Always keep one hand on your baby and never leave them unattended in the bath. Use a small baby tub or sink with a non-slip surface, and fill it with just a few inches of warm water;

around 98-100°F is ideal. Test the water temperature with your wrist or elbow to ensure it's comfortable. Supporting your baby's head and keeping a firm but gentle grip helps them feel secure. Bathing two to three times a week is sufficient, as more frequent bathing can dry out your baby's delicate skin.

Bath time isn't just about cleanliness. Ensure your touch is gentle and soothing; this is an opportunity to create a calm and nurturing environment where your baby feels safe and loved. Speak softly to your baby, maintain eye contact, and enjoy this special time together. Each bath is a time to care for your baby's physical needs and a chance to bond, watching them discover the simple joy of warm water and your comforting presence.

Baby Sleep Patterns: Establishing Healthy Routines

In the early days with your newborn, you might wonder if you'll ever sleep through the night again. Newborns have unique sleep cycles, often waking every few hours to feed, which is entirely normal. These tiny beings spend about 16 to 17 hours a day sleeping but in short bursts of time. They haven't yet learned the difference between day and night, leading to what some call day-night confusion. As the months pass, you'll notice changes in their sleep patterns. By around three to six months, many babies begin to sleep for longer stretches at night, and the number of daytime naps will gradually decrease. Understanding these shifts can help you adjust your expectations and find ways to manage your own rest.

Establishing a consistent sleep routine is one of the most effective ways to encourage healthy sleep habits in your baby. Begin by setting a predictable bedtime routine that signals to your baby that it's time to wind down. This might include activities like a warm bath, a gentle massage, or a bedtime story. Creating a sleep-conducive environment is equally important. Ensure the room is quiet, dark, and at a comfortable temperature between 68 and 72 degrees Fahrenheit is ideal. Consider using blackout curtains to block out light and a white noise machine to drown out household sounds. These minor adjustments can significantly affect how quickly and soundly your baby falls asleep.

Sleep disruptions are a common challenge, but there are strategies to help you navigate them. Night-waking and sleep regressions can occur as your baby grows and develops new skills. During these times, try to remain patient and consistent with your routine. Techniques for soothing a fussy baby include gentle rocking, a calming lullaby, or offering a pacifier. Pacifiers can be a double-edged sword; while they provide comfort and help some babies self-soothe, they can also become a dependency. If kept for too long, they can affect oral development. Weighing the pros and cons is essential, and let the decision be based on what works best for your family.

Safety is paramount when it comes to your baby's sleep. Follow the ABCs of safe sleep: your baby should sleep Alone, on their Back, and in a crib or bassinet. Avoid soft bedding, pillows, and toys in the crib to reduce the risk of suffocation. Co-sleeping is a topic of much debate. While it can foster closeness, it also poses risks, so if you decide to co-sleep, ensure you follow guidelines to minimize hazards. As your baby grows, transitioning from a bassinet to a crib can be a big step. Making this transition smoother involves maintaining the familiar elements of their sleep routine and providing comfort and security in their new sleeping environment.

I chose to have a bassinet that rested next to my bed, almost like an extension of the bed. It was the best of both worlds: I could be close to my son but also keep him safe with his own proper bedding, and I never had to get out of bed for feedings. The main downside to this plan was that it made for an extremely difficult transition to independent sleep. Honestly, all options have pros and cons.

Gentle sleep training methods can help develop healthy sleep habits over time. Approaches such as the Ferber or the fading method involve gradual adjustments to how you respond to your baby's cries, helping them learn to self-soothe. Recognizing and responding to sleep cues, such as rubbing their eyes or yawning, can help you put your baby to bed before they become overtired. Each baby is different, and finding the right balance between comforting your child and allowing them to learn independent sleep skills is key.

Swaddling and Diapering: Techniques and Tips

Swaddling is a time-honored technique that can provide comfort and security, mimicking the snug environment of the womb. When done correctly, swaddling can soothe a fussy baby and promote better sleep. To swaddle safely, lay a blanket flat and fold one corner. Place your baby on their back with their head above the fold. Wrap one side of the blanket snugly across your baby's chest, tucking it under their body. Fold the bottom of the blanket up over their feet, then wrap the remaining side securely. Ensure the swaddle is snug but not too tight, allowing enough room for your baby to move their hips and legs freely. As your baby grows, you'll need to transition out of swaddling, typically around two months, when they start showing signs of rolling over. Gradually leave one arm out of the swaddle, then both, allowing them to adjust to sleeping without constraints.

In the beginning, parenthood will feel like a vast world lined with… Diapers! Diapering will quickly become a daunting yet fundamental task. Whether you choose cloth or disposable diapers, each has its benefits and considerations. Cloth diapers are reusable, eco-friendly, and gentle on your baby's skin. They require regular washing but can lead to long-term savings. Disposable diapers, on the other hand, offer convenience with ease of use and disposability, often proving to be more absorbent. The choice usually boils down to personal preference, lifestyle, and environmental considerations.

Whichever you opt for, preventing and treating diaper rash is crucial. Ensure frequent diaper changes to keep your baby's skin dry and clean. Applying a barrier cream can protect sensitive skin from irritation. Allowing some diaper-free time can also give your baby's skin a chance to breathe, reducing the risk of rashes. Newborn poop goes through several distinct stages as their digestive system adjusts to life outside the womb. The following list will help shed light on the most common poop curiosities parents have and what to expect:

1. Meconium (Days 1-2)

In the first couple of days after birth, your baby's poop will be meconium, a dark green or black, sticky, tar-like substance. Meconium is made up of amniotic fluid, mucus, skin cells, and other materials ingested while in the womb. Its appearance signals that your baby's digestive system is working correctly.

2. Transitional Poop (Days 3-4)

As your baby begins feeding, their poop transitions from meconium to a lighter, thinner consistency. The color will shift to a greenish-brown or mustard-yellow, and it may look less sticky. This stage indicates that your baby is starting to digest milk or formula effectively.

3. Breastfed Baby Poop

For breastfed babies, poop becomes yellow or mustard-colored, with a seedy or curd-like texture. It's often loose and watery, almost resembling diarrhea but without a foul odor. Breastfed babies may poop frequently in the first few weeks (after nearly every feeding) or less often as they grow and their digestion adjusts.

4. Formula-Fed Baby Poop

Formula-fed babies tend to have firmer, tan, or yellow-brown stools compared to breastfed babies. The consistency may resemble peanut butter, and the smell can be slightly more pungent. Formula-fed babies usually poop less frequently than breastfed ones, often once a day or every couple of days.

5. Solid Food Poop (Around 4-6 Months)

When your baby starts eating solid foods, their poop will undergo another transformation. It may become thicker, more formed, and vary in color depending on the foods they eat (e.g., orange for carrots and green for peas). The smell will also become more pungent as their digestive system processes a more complex diet.

When to Be Concerned

While these stages are normal, certain signs may warrant a call to your pediatrician:

• Black poop after the first few days (could indicate blood).

• White or pale stools (may indicate a liver issue).

• Red streaks (possible blood from irritation or allergy).

• Persistent diarrhea or constipation.

Monitoring your baby's poop is a helpful way to track their digestion and overall health as they grow! Now, let's dive into the dirty deed. Diaper changing for boys and girls follows the same general steps, but there are a few key differences to keep in mind to ensure cleanliness and prevent discomfort or infections.

Diaper Changing a Boy

1 Watch Out for Spray: Baby boys often urinate during diaper changes, so be prepared with a cloth or new diaper to cover their penis while cleaning.

2 Clean Thoroughly Around the Penis and Scrotum: Gently wipe from front to back, ensuring all creases and folds are clean. Avoid retracting the foreskin if your baby is uncircumcised, as it will naturally separate over time.

3 Positioning the Penis: When putting on a new diaper, ensure the penis is pointing downward to prevent leaks out the top or sides of the diaper.

4 Extra Padding for Boys: Boys may need a snugger diaper fit or a slightly more absorbent diaper due to their concentrated urination.

Diaper Changing a Girl

1 Front-to-Back Cleaning: Always wipe from front to back to prevent bacteria from entering the vaginal area, which can lead to urinary tract infections (UTIs).

2 Cleaning Folds and Creases: Gently clean all folds in the genital area, as poop or residue can easily get trapped.

3 Avoid Over-Cleaning: Baby girls have a natural discharge that helps keep their vagina healthy, so avoid scrubbing or using wipes unnecessarily in this area.

4 Be Aware of Normal Vaginal Discharge: It's normal for newborn girls to have a small amount of white or even blood-tinged discharge due to maternal hormones; this usually resolves within the first few weeks.

Common Considerations for Both

• **Frequent Changes**: Change diapers regularly to prevent diaper rash.

• **Use Barrier Creams**: Apply a thin layer of diaper cream to protect the skin, especially if your baby has sensitive skin.

• **Choose the Right Diaper Size**: Proper fit helps prevent leaks and irritation.

Paying attention to these minor differences ensures that diaper changes are safe, hygienic, and comfortable for your baby, regardless of gender.

Common concerns about diapering and swaddling often stem from ensuring your baby's comfort and safety. A properly fitting diaper should be snug but not restrictive, with tabs fastened symmetrically. Check that the diaper's waistband and leg cuffs are flat, as any folds can cause leaks. With swaddling, overheating is a risk to be mindful of. Use lightweight, breathable fabrics and keep the room at a comfortable temperature. Monitoring your baby's temperature by feeling the back of their neck can help ensure they're not too warm. If you're unsure, consider using a sleep sack, which offers the security of swaddling without the risk of overheating.

Additional products can enhance your diapering and swaddling routine. A well-stocked diaper bag is indispensable, containing necessities like wipes, diaper cream, and a portable changing pad. Swaddling blankets made from stretchy fabrics or those with Velcro or snap closures can simplify the swaddling process. Sleep sacks, which are wearable blankets, offer a safe alternative as your baby transitions from swaddling. These tools not only make the process more efficient but also add an element of ease to your daily routine.

Baby Milestones: What to Expect in the First Year

As you watch your baby grow, each day brings new surprises and achievements. By the end of the first month, your baby might lift their head briefly during tummy time. By three months, you may see your little one smiling at familiar faces, a heartwarming moment that signifies social development. Around four to six months, many babies start to roll over, a significant physical milestone. By the time they reach nine months, some will begin crawling, exploring their environment with curiosity. Approaching the one-year mark, your baby might attempt those first wobbly steps, transitioning from crawling to walking. Alongside these physical milestones, cognitive and social development unfolds as your baby begins to babble, play peek-a-boo, and mimic sounds. These milestones are guideposts, reflecting your baby's growth and development during this transformative year.

Supporting your baby's development involves engaging them in activities that promote learning and growth. Tummy time is essential, as it strengthens neck and shoulder muscles, preparing your baby for crawling and sitting. Encourage your baby to reach for toys during tummy time, fostering hand-eye coordination. Try to have Interactive play, such as singing or playing with colorful blocks; it stimulates cognitive development. Reading to your baby, even at an early age, develops language skills and introduces them to the rhythm and melody of spoken words. The sound of your voice and the closeness of these moments also strengthen your bond. Simple activities like these provide a foundation for learning and exploration, nurturing your baby's innate curiosity.

It's natural to wonder if your baby is reaching milestones "on time." However, it's crucial to remember that each baby develops at their own pace. Some may achieve milestones sooner, while others take their time. This variation is perfectly normal and reflects individual differences. If you're concerned about developmental delays, consult your pediatrician. They can offer guidance and, if necessary, suggest interventions to support your baby's development. Look for signs such as lack of eye contact or not responding to sounds, as these might warrant a professional opinion. Trust your instincts; you know your baby best, and early intervention can be beneficial if needed.

Celebrating milestones, no matter how small is an opportunity to acknowledge your baby's progress and your role in nurturing their growth. Consider keeping a milestone journal, capturing these precious moments in words and photos. This journal becomes a keepsake, a testament to your baby's evolution. Sharing these milestones with family and friends allows them to partake in the joy and wonder of your baby's growth. Every smile, step, and sound is a victory, a reminder of the miracle of development.

As you witness these milestones, remember that each one marks a step forward. Your support, love, and encouragement have been essential to their growth, so celebrate each achievement you've shared.

Each chapter builds on the last, equipping you with the knowledge and tools to get through the postpartum period. In this chapter, we discussed nurturing your baby's development, but as you continue reading, you'll gain insights into nurturing your own. Let's lay the foundation and ensure that you maintain health and happiness.

NUTRITION AND LIFESTYLE ADJUSTMENTS

Y ou're sitting at your kitchen table, the morning light filtering
through the window as you sip a warm cup of tea. Your baby
is napping, and for a moment, you have a chance to reflect on your
own needs. Nutrition often takes a backseat when your main focus
is being a mom. Yet, it is the cornerstone of your recovery, providing
the fuel your body needs to heal and regain strength. Just as your
baby requires nourishment to grow, you, too, need a balanced diet to
support you during this time. A diet rich in essential nutrients can
aid in healing, help regulate energy levels, and bolster your overall
well-being, making each day more manageable.

The role of macronutrients in postpartum recovery is vital. Proteins,
carbohydrates, and fats each play a unique part in rebuilding your
body. Proteins serve as the building blocks essential for tissue repair
and hormone production. Lean meats, fish, eggs, and legumes are
excellent sources. Carbohydrates provide the energy needed to
tackle the demands of motherhood; whole grains, fruits, and vegetables can keep you feeling energized throughout the day. Healthy fats,
found in salmon, avocados, nuts, and olive oil, support brain func-

tion and help absorb vitamins. These macronutrients should form the foundation of your meals, offering a balance that sustains you.

In addition to macronutrients, certain vitamins and minerals are crucial for postpartum health. Iron is vital, particularly after childbirth, as it replenishes blood loss and combats fatigue. Foods like spinach, lentils, and lean red meat are rich in iron. Pairing them with vitamin C-rich foods like citrus fruits enhances absorption. Calcium and vitamin D are equally important, supporting bone health and aiding in the recovery of your musculoskeletal system. Dairy products, fortified plant milks, and leafy greens are excellent sources. Incorporating these nutrients into your diet ensures your body receives the support it needs to recover and thrive.

Creating a balanced postpartum diet involves building a plate that reflects variety and balance. Aim for colorful meals, incorporating a spectrum of fruits and vegetables. This ensures a range of nutrients and makes meals more appealing and satisfying. Incorporate nutrient-dense snacks to bridge the gap between meals. Think of a handful of almonds, a slice of whole-grain toast with nut butter, or yogurt with fresh berries. These snacks provide a quick energy boost and keep hunger at bay, allowing you to focus on your baby without feeling depleted.

However, maintaining a healthy diet in the postpartum period comes with its own set of challenges. Time constraints are a common hurdle, as the demands of a newborn leave little room for meal preparation. Consider preparing simple dishes that require minimal effort. A stir-fry with pre-cut vegetables, tofu, or chicken can be whipped up in minutes. Appetite changes and cravings may also arise, influenced by hormonal shifts and sleep deprivation. Listen to your body, honoring hunger cues and opting for nourishing options. Keeping a variety of healthy snacks accessible can help manage cravings and prevent reaching for less nutritious choices.

Reflection Section: Crafting Your Nutrition Plan

Take a moment to reflect on your current eating habits. Consider what foods energize you and which leave you feeling sluggish. Use this reflection to guide your meal planning, focusing on incorporating more of the foods that uplift you. Jot down a list of go-to snacks and meals that align with your nutritional goals, making it easier to stay on track even on the busiest days.

As you navigate this chapter of nutrition and lifestyle adjustments, remember that nourishing yourself is an act of self-love. It equips you with the strength and vitality needed to embrace the joys and challenges of motherhood with resilience and grace.

Meal Planning for Busy Moms: Quick and Nutritious

It's mid-afternoon, and your baby is finally down for a nap. You have a moment to yourself and realize you haven't eaten a proper meal all day. Meal planning can be a lifesaver in these moments, offering structure amidst the unpredictability of new motherhood. By planning meals, you can streamline grocery shopping, ensuring you have all the ingredients you need without the stress of last-minute trips to the store. This foresight saves time and ensures that you and your family have consistent access to nutritious meals. A well-thought-out meal plan reduces the daily stress of deciding what to cook, allowing you to focus more on your recovery and your baby.

Creating efficient meal plans involves some strategic thinking and a bit of creativity. Batch cooking and meal prepping can transform your approach to food, allowing you to prepare multiple meals in one go. Consider dedicating a few hours on the weekend to cooking large portions of staples like grains, roasted vegetables, or proteins. You can then mix and match these ingredients throughout the week, creating a variety of dishes without starting from scratch each day. Utilizing leftovers creatively can also stretch your efforts further. For instance, a roast chicken can become a chicken salad sandwich one day and a hearty soup the next. This saves time and adds variety to your meals, keeping them exciting and diverse.

Simplicity is key When looking for quick and nutritious meal ideas. One-pot meals are a fantastic option, requiring minimal preparation and cleanup like a pot of chili simmering on the stove, filled with beans, lean meat, and vegetables, providing a balanced blend of protein, fiber, and vitamins. Or consider a stir-fry with colorful bell peppers, broccoli, and tofu tossed in a light soy sauce, served over rice. Smoothies are another quick option, packed with nutrients and easily customizable. Blend spinach, a banana, a handful of berries, and a scoop of yogurt for a refreshing and nourishing drink you can enjoy on the go. These meals are designed to support your recovery without demanding too much of your time or energy.

Technology can be a helpful ally in meal planning, offering tools to organize and simplify the process. Meal planning apps, such as Pepperplate or Meal Garden, allow you to import recipes, create shopping lists, and plan meals on a calendar accessible from multiple devices. These apps streamline the planning process, making it easier to track what you need and when you need it. Recipe databases and online communities are treasure troves of inspiration, offering a wealth of ideas to suit any dietary preference or restriction. Engaging with these resources can spark creativity and introduce new flavors to your kitchen.

Embracing meal planning as part of your routine can create a more predictable rhythm in your day. It allows you to focus on nourishing yourself and provides the energy to care for your growing family. By planning, you give yourself the gift of less stress and more time to enjoy the moments that truly matter.

Hydration and Its Importance: Staying Energized

You're in the middle of a busy day, juggling baby care, household duties, and maybe even some work. With all the hustle, it's easy to overlook something as simple as drinking water. Yet, hydration is a cornerstone of your postpartum recovery. Your body, still recovering from childbirth, relies on adequate fluid intake to function optimally. Water plays a crucial role in facilitating digestion and nutrient absorption, ensuring that your body can effectively utilize the nutrients from your diet. When breastfeeding, staying hydrated is even more critical; breast milk is about 90% water, so keeping your fluid levels up supports milk production and maintains your energy levels. Think of each glass of water as a small but mighty tool in your recovery toolkit, helping you rebuild and rejuvenate.

To maintain proper hydration levels, aim to drink about eight to ten glasses of water daily, adjusting based on your activity level and climate. An easy way to monitor your hydration is by checking the color of your urine; pale yellow indicates adequate hydration, while darker shades suggest you need more fluids. Dehydration can manifest in various ways, including headaches, fatigue, and dry skin. By recognizing these signs, you can take immediate steps to rehydrate, ensuring your body functions smoothly. Carrying a reusable water bottle is a simple yet effective strategy to keep hydration at the forefront of your mind. It serves as a visual reminder to take regular sips throughout the day, whether nursing, playing with your baby, or catching a quick break.

Beyond plain water, hydrating foods and beverages can enhance fluid intake. Herbal teas, like chamomile or peppermint, offer a soothing alternative to water, providing warmth and comfort while keeping you hydrated. Flavored naturally with slices of cucumber, lemon, or berries, infused water can make drinking water more enjoyable and encourage you to consume more. High-water-content fruits and vegetables like watermelon, cucumbers, and oranges are delicious and hydrating. Including these in your snacks or meals adds variety and helps meet your hydration needs effortlessly. Imagine a refreshing salad with crisp lettuce, juicy tomatoes, and cool cucumber slices; each bite contributes to your daily fluid intake.

Maintaining consistent hydration can be challenging, especially when you're busy caring for a newborn. Setting reminders to drink water can be helpful. Use your phone or a simple kitchen timer to prompt you every hour or so. Associating water intake with routine activities, like feeding your baby or preparing meals, can create a habit that ensures you stay hydrated without extra effort. For new mothers, hydration is not just about quenching thirst; it's about supporting your body's intricate systems, from digestion to lactation.

Sleep Strategies for Moms: Prioritizing Rest

In the haze of new motherhood, sleep often becomes a precious commodity. The unique sleep needs of postpartum mothers cannot be overstated. Restorative sleep is crucial for healing, both physically and mentally. It plays a significant role in tissue repair, hormone regulation, and emotional balance. However, the reality of nighttime feedings, diaper changes, and a baby's unpredictable sleep schedule can make uninterrupted sleep seem like a distant memory. Coping with disrupted sleep patterns requires a blend of strategy and flexibility. It's about finding small moments throughout the day to recharge, recognizing that rest may come in snippets rather than long stretches.

Creating a sleep-conducive environment is a practical step toward better rest. Consider the bedroom a sanctuary designed to promote relaxation and slumber. Blackout curtains can block out intrusive light, creating a dark haven that signals to your body it's time to wind down. Just like your baby, you can also use a white noise machine to drown out household sounds, providing a consistent and soothing backdrop for sleep. Keeping the room cool enhances comfort, as a slight drop in temperature signals the body to prepare for rest. These adjustments, though small, can create an atmosphere that encourages deeper, more restful sleep, even if only for brief intervals.

Establishing a sleep routine can signal to your body that it's time to unwind. Consistency is key; try to set regular sleep and wake times, aligning them with your baby's schedule when possible. This rhythm helps regulate your internal clock, making falling asleep and waking up easier. Before bed, engage in relaxation techniques that promote calmness. A warm bath, gentle stretching, or reading a book can ease the transition from the day's busyness to the night's tranquility. These rituals act as cues, telling your body that it's time to relax and prepare for rest.

Overcoming sleep challenges requires a blend of creativity and collaboration. Napping strategies can be your ally, offering restorative pockets of rest. Nap when your baby naps, even if it's just for 20 minutes. These short bursts of sleep can rejuvenate your energy levels and improve mental clarity. Sharing nighttime responsibilities with a partner is another effective strategy. Take turns handling feedings or diaper changes, allowing each of you to enjoy a more extended period of uninterrupted sleep. This teamwork distributes the workload and strengthens your partnership, providing mutual support during this demanding time. Some families opt to have a night nurse to help with baby care at night so both parents can sleep.

Remember, prioritizing rest is not a luxury; it's a necessity. By creating a supportive sleep environment, establishing a routine, and embracing flexible strategies, you can handle the challenges of postpartum sleep with greater ease. Your body is healing, adjusting, and adapting, and it deserves the care and attention that comes with quality rest. As you focus on nurturing your own sleep needs, you're better equipped to care for your baby, approach each day with renewed energy, and savor the precious moments of early motherhood.

Incorporating Physical Activity: Fun and Family-Friendly

Physical activity after childbirth is not just about regaining physical strength; it's a pillar for mental health and emotional well-being. Exercise releases endorphins, those wonderful chemicals that boost your mood and energy levels, helping you feel more grounded. It's also a fantastic way to manage weight and rebuild strength. While your body has been through significant changes, engaging in regular physical activity can help you reconnect with it, fostering a sense of empowerment and resilience.

Finding ways to include physical activity with your baby can be a joyful experience, transforming exercise into a bonding opportunity. Try baby-wearing walks, where your little one cozily snuggles against you in a carrier, allowing you to enjoy the benefits of walking while keeping your baby close. The gentle rhythm of your steps can soothe them, making it a peaceful outing for both of you. Stroller exercises offer another option, turning a simple walk into a full-body workout. Incorporate lunges or squats during your stroll, adding a bit of fun to the routine. Parent-and-baby yoga classes have grown popular, offering a space to stretch, breathe, and relax while engaging your baby in gentle poses. These activities support your physical health and nurture a deeper connection with your child.

Integrating exercise into your busy schedule may seem daunting, but with a little creativity, it's entirely possible. Short workouts during nap times can be incredibly effective. A 10-minute routine focusing on core strength or flexibility can make a significant difference. Use household chores as opportunities for movement; vacuuming, gardening, or even dancing around the living room can elevate your heart rate and enhance fitness. The key is to view these everyday tasks as part of your exercise regimen, blending them into your routine seamlessly. This approach not only makes exercise more accessible but also adds an element of enjoyment to daily responsibilities.

Setting realistic fitness goals and tracking your progress is crucial for maintaining motivation and creating a section in your journal for fitness. It can be an inspiring way to document your progress. Record your workouts, note how you feel afterward and set small, achievable goals. These might include increasing the duration of your walks or trying a new class. As you reach these milestones, celebrate each victory, no matter how small. Treat yourself to a new pair of leggings or a relaxing bath. These celebrations reinforce your accomplishments, keeping you motivated and engaged.

Embracing exercise is a gift to yourself that offers strength and joy. You're building a foundation for your health and the bond you share with your family, creating memories that will last a lifetime. In the next chapter, we'll explore mental health and discuss the emotional aspects of the fourth trimester.

MENTAL HEALTH AND EMOTIONAL WELL-BEING

E nvision yourself sitting in your favorite chair, cradling your newborn, yet feeling a cloud hanging over you that you can't shake off. Your heart should be bursting with joy, but instead, a persistent sadness seems to cling to every moment. It's a reality that many new mothers face, often without warning. This isn't just a fleeting case of the baby blues that passes with a good night's sleep. Postpartum depression (PPD) is a more complex mix of physical, emotional, and behavioral changes that can overshadow the joy of new motherhood. Understanding this condition is critical, not only for your well-being but also for your ability to care for your baby. Recognizing the signs early can make a world of difference.

Recognizing Postpartum Depression: Signs and Solutions

Postpartum depression differs from the typical baby blues, which many women experience shortly after birth. While the blues might manifest as brief periods of moodiness and sadness, PPD is more severe and long-lasting. Persistent sadness or mood swings are common indicators. You might notice a lack of interest in activities that once brought you joy. This withdrawal can feel isolating, adding to the burden of the condition. Changes in appetite and sleep patterns are also prevalent. You might find yourself unable to sleep when the baby sleeps, or perhaps you're sleeping more than usual yet never feel rested. These changes can exacerbate feelings of fatigue and hopelessness, creating a vicious cycle that seems impossible to break.

A framework for self-assessment can be an empowering tool for understanding your mental health. Simple questionnaires, often available online or through your healthcare provider, can help you evaluate your feelings and identify whether they align with symptoms of PPD. Being honest in your responses is key. These assessments provide a starting point, but knowing when to consult a healthcare provider is crucial. If your feelings of sadness or anxiety persist beyond two weeks, or if they interfere with your daily activities and ability to care for your baby, it's time to reach out for professional help. You deserve to feel supported and understood; seeking help is a brave step towards healing.

Various treatment options are available for postpartum depression, allowing you to choose a path that suits your needs. Psychotherapy, often referred to as talk therapy, is a highly effective method. You might find comfort in speaking with a counselor or therapist who can help you navigate your feelings and develop coping strategies. Medication is another option, often used in conjunction with therapy under the supervision of a healthcare provider. It's important to discuss potential benefits and risks with your doctor, ensuring that any medication prescribed aligns with your personal and medical needs. Seeking therapy or medication is a sign of strength, a commitment to your health and well-being. Also, as mentioned before, many medications for postpartum depression are compatible with breastfeeding by having either minimal transfer into breast milk or a low risk of side effects for the baby.

Support networks play a vital role in recovery. Family and friends can provide a safety net, offering emotional support and practical assistance. Sharing your feelings with those close to you can alleviate the sense of isolation. Let them know how they can help, whether watching the baby for an hour while you rest or simply lending an ear. Support groups, both in-person and online, offer a community of people who understand your experiences. These groups provide a space to share stories, exchange advice, and find solace in knowing you are not alone. Building a supportive network requires reaching out, but the benefits are immeasurable.

Reflection Section: Building Your Support Network

Take a moment to consider your current support system. Who in your life can you rely on for emotional support? Are there friends or family members who have offered help? List their names and think about how you might reach out to them. Consider joining a local or online support group. These connections can be a source of strength, offering understanding and empathy when it's needed most. Reaching out can be daunting, but remember, you are creating a circle of care that will uplift you during this challenging time.

Understanding and addressing postpartum depression is an essential step in nurturing both your well-being and your relationship with your baby. By recognizing the signs, seeking appropriate treatments, and building a strong support network, you can navigate this challenging period with resilience and hope. Remember, you are not alone in this, and with the proper support, you can find your way back to joy and fulfillment.

Anxiety Management: Techniques for New Moms

Anxiety is a frequent visitor for many new mothers, often lurking in the shadows of everyday life. It might manifest as a racing heart, sweaty palms, or an overwhelming sense of dread. Common triggers include concerns about your baby's health, adjusting to new responsibilities, or even the pressure of meeting the expectations you've set for yourself. These feelings can seep into your bond with your baby, making interactions tense and strained instead of joyful and nurturing. Anxiety is a common theme of motherhood, and sadly, it never truly goes away. I've heard countless stories of mothers watching their babies sleep so peacefully that they fear they aren't breathing, so they startle them awake just to be safe. Or envision themselves tripping down the stairs while carrying their baby. If I had a penny for every random imaginary dread I've experienced with motherhood, I'd be a billionaire. Understanding the prevalence and impact of anxiety is the first step in reclaiming your peace of mind.

Luckily, some practical techniques can offer relief. Just as it was helpful with managing those postpartum emotional swings, deep breathing can also be beneficial in handling anxiety. When you feel anxiety creeping in, pause and focus on your breath. Inhale slowly through your nose, allowing your belly to rise, then exhale gently through your mouth. This simple act can calm your nervous system and bring clarity in overwhelming moments. Progressive muscle relaxation is another strategy worth exploring. It involves tensing and relaxing each muscle group, from your toes to your head. This practice alleviates physical tension and helps center your thoughts, creating a sense of calm and control.

Another trick for thwarting the anticipation of the unknown is creating a routine. Incorporating structure into your daily life can be a powerful ally against anxiety. While flexibility is key, having a consistent schedule can provide a sense of predictability and security. Start by crafting a routine that includes time for relaxation. Perhaps it's a quiet moment with your morning coffee or a walk with your baby in the afternoon sun. These pockets of peace can act as anchors, grounding you in the present and allowing your mind to unwind. By establishing a rhythm to your day, you create an environment that supports emotional stability and reduces the likelihood of anxiety taking hold.

Open communication is vital in managing anxiety. Sharing your feelings with someone you trust can alleviate the burden of carrying them alone. Talk to your partner or a close friend about what you're experiencing. Their support and understanding can provide comfort and offer new perspectives. If anxiety feels too overwhelming, as stated before, seeking professional advice is a wise step. A therapist can help you explore the roots of your anxiety and develop personalized strategies to manage it. Remember, reaching out for help is an act of strength, not weakness. You deserve to feel supported and understood as you wade through these turbulent waters.

Cognitive Behavioral Therapy: Tools for Reframing Thoughts

Cognitive Behavioral Therapy, often referred to as CBT is a practical, evidence-based approach that helps you explore and reshape the thoughts that might be clouding your postpartum experience. At its core, CBT is about recognizing the patterns in your thoughts and understanding how they influence your emotions and behaviors. You might find yourself caught in a cycle of negative thoughts, like believing you're not doing enough as a mother, which can lead to feelings of inadequacy and anxiety. Understanding these thought patterns is the first step in breaking free from them. CBT encourages you to identify these negative cycles and provides tools to challenge and change them, offering a pathway to cultivate a healthier mindset.

One of the most effective tools in CBT is the use of thought records. This involves keeping a journal where you document specific thoughts that arise throughout your day, particularly those that trigger negative emotions. By writing down these thoughts, you can begin to identify recurring patterns and evaluate their validity. For instance, you might note a moment when you felt like a failure because your baby was fussy. In your journal, you can examine this thought critically, asking yourself if it's based on evidence or a distorted perception. Over time, you'll learn to reframe these thoughts, replacing them with more balanced and constructive ones. This process, known as cognitive restructuring, empowers you to transform unhelpful thoughts into positive reflections. Here are some simplified steps:

1 Identify the Negative Thought

• The process begins by recognizing automatic thoughts that arise in response to situations. These thoughts are often distorted, irrational, or overly pessimistic.

• Example: After a difficult event, you might think, "I always mess things up."

2 Evaluate the Thought

• Once a thought is identified, you assess its accuracy and usefulness.

• Ask yourself, "Is this thought based on facts or assumptions?"

• Now, what evidence supports or contradicts this thought?

• Now ask, "Am I overgeneralizing, catastrophizing, or using all-or-nothing thinking?"

3 Challenge the Thought

• Replace distorted thoughts with more balanced, rational ones.

○ Example: Original Thought: "I always mess things up."

○ Evidence: "I made a mistake but handled other parts well."

○ Revised Thought: "I'm not perfect, but I'm learning and improving."

4 Replace the Thought with Positive, Realistic Thoughts

• Create new, healthier ways of thinking that better reflect reality.

• Example: Instead of "I'm a failure," you might think, "I had a setback, but I can work through it."

5 Repeat and Reinforce the Process

• Cognitive restructuring requires practice and repetition. Over time, these healthier thought patterns become more automatic.

Developing healthier thought patterns is a gradual process that involves nurturing positive mental habits. Practicing gratitude can be a powerful way to shift your focus from what's going wrong to what's going right. Consider starting each day by listing three things you're grateful for, no matter how small they may seem. This simple exercise can help you cultivate a mindset of appreciation, which can enhance your overall well-being. Positive affirmations are another tool at your disposal. By repeating affirmations like "I am a capable and loving mother," you can reinforce a positive self-image and counteract negative self-talk. Setting realistic goals and expectations for yourself is also crucial. Recognize that it's okay to have setbacks and that progress doesn't have to be linear. Setting achievable goals creates a sense of accomplishment that fuels your motivation and confidence.

While self-guided CBT exercises can be incredibly beneficial, there may be times when professional guidance is needed. As stated before, seeking the expertise of a qualified therapist can provide you with tailored support and deeper insights into your thought patterns. If the above exercises resonate with you, try finding a therapist that specializes in CBT. They can work with you to develop a personalized plan, offering strategies and exercises that align with your specific needs and unique pressures. If in-person sessions are challenging to attend, exploring online CBT resources can be a convenient alternative. Many platforms offer virtual therapy sessions and self-help modules that you can access from the comfort of your home.

CBT is not just about managing negative thoughts; it's about building a foundation for your emotional growth. By actively engaging with these techniques, you can create a more positive narrative for yourself as a new mother.

Mindfulness Practices: Staying Present Amidst Chaos

Your mind might be racing with thoughts of to-dos and worries, but allow mindfulness to become a sanctuary. Mindfulness is about being present and fully immersed in the moment without judgment. For new mothers, it offers a pathway to enhance emotional well-being. Mindfulness reduces stress and sharpens your focus by focusing on the present, allowing you to connect more deeply with your child. It encourages you to savor the small and beautiful moments with your baby. This practice does not require hours of meditation but can be woven into the fabric of your day-to-day life, offering peace.

Simple mindfulness exercises can seamlessly integrate into your daily routine, no matter how hectic. Start with mindful breathing, a powerful technique that anchors you to the present. Find a comfortable position, close your eyes, and take a deep breath through your nose, letting it fill your lungs. Hold for a moment, then exhale slowly through your mouth. As you breathe, focus on the sensation of the air moving in and out. This practice can be done anywhere—while feeding your baby, taking a shower, or even during those precious moments when your baby naps. Another effective exercise is the body scan meditation. Lie down in a comfortable position, and slowly direct your attention to each part of your body, starting from your toes and moving up to your head. Notice any sensations, tension, or areas of relaxation. This exercise promotes physical relaxation and cultivates a sense of awareness and connection with your body.

The role of mindfulness in stress reduction cannot be overstated. It offers a gentle yet powerful way to manage stress, promoting relaxation and emotional balance. Mindful eating, for example, transforms a routine task into a moment of awareness and appreciation. As you eat, focus on the flavors, textures, and sensations, turning each bite into an experience. This simple act can ground you, providing a respite from all your flooding thoughts.

Similarly, mindful walking can be a meditative practice. As you walk, pay attention to the sensation of your feet touching the ground, the rhythm of your steps, and the movement of your body. These practices help you handle challenging emotions by creating a space where you can observe and respond with calmness rather than reacting impulsively.

Consistency is key to reaping the long-term benefits of mindfulness. It's about making mindfulness a habit, a natural part of your daily life. Set aside a few minutes each day for mindfulness exercises, gradually increasing the duration as you become more comfortable with the practice. Choose a specific morning or evening time to create a routine. Incorporate mindfulness into daily activities, whether during a feeding session, while taking a walk, or even during a hectic day. However, flexibility should be remembered. The goal is not to add another task to your list but to enrich your life with moments of presence and peace. Over time, these practices can transform your experience of motherhood, helping you move through any challenge with grace.

Self-Compassion: Embracing Your New Identity

As a new mother, it's easy to fall into the trap of self-criticism. Thoughts of "I should be doing more" or "Why can't I handle this better?" are all too common. This is where self-compassion becomes a powerful ally. It's about treating yourself with the same kindness and understanding you would offer a friend. In the postpartum period, self-compassion is vital. Where self-criticism berates, self-kindness nurtures. This mindset shift recognizes that everyone struggles and makes mistakes, and that's okay. It's a shared human experience, one that connects us all in our imperfections.

Cultivating self-compassion doesn't happen overnight, but with intentionality, it becomes part of your daily life. Start by practicing self-kindness through affirmations. Look in the mirror and tell yourself, "I am enough" or "I am learning each day." These simple phrases reinforce a positive self-image. When moments of doubt or frustration arise, try self-soothing techniques. It could be as simple as wrapping yourself in a cozy blanket or taking a warm bath. These acts of comfort remind you that you deserve care and gentleness. Another helpful tool is the practice of loving-kindness meditation. Close your eyes, take a deep breath, and silently repeat phrases like, "May I be happy, may I be healthy, may I live with ease." This meditation fosters a sense of warmth and compassion towards yourself, creating a foundation of self-love that supports you through trials and triumphs.

Self-compassion holds the power to transform your mental health. As you embrace your new identity, feelings of inadequacy and guilt often surface. Self-compassion acts as a balm, soothing these wounds. When you speak kindly to yourself, you reduce the harshness of self-criticism, allowing room for healing and growth. This practice doesn't just alleviate negative feelings; it enhances resilience. With self-compassion, you build an emotional balance that endures through sleepless nights and challenging days. You become more adaptable and better able to face whatever motherhood throws your way. This emotional stability benefits you and radiates to those around you, including your baby, fostering a nurturing environment filled with love and acceptance.

Reflective activities are invaluable for deepening your practice of self-compassion. Consider including a place in your journal where you explore your thoughts and feelings. Use prompts like, "What are three things I appreciate about myself today?" or "How can I show myself kindness in this moment?" These reflections increase self-awareness and foster acceptance. Journaling becomes a safe space to express vulnerabilities and celebrate strengths.

Remember that self-compassion is not a luxury; it's a necessity. It empowers you to embrace your new identity with grace and understanding. By practicing self-kindness and engaging in reflective exercises, you nurture your heart. This heart becomes your compass, guiding you through the complexities of motherhood with strength and love.

In this chapter, we explored how nurturing your mental and emotional health can profoundly influence your experience as a new mother. Now, let's further support your inner needs by embracing self-care.

MAKE A DIFFERENCE WITH YOUR REVIEW

Your words can help a new mom feel supported on her postpartum journey.

The Complete Postpartum Handbook was created to make the fourth trimester easier. A quick review can help another mom find the guidance she needs.

Share your experience
Scan the QR Code here

Thank you for being part of this mission!

Warmly,

Evelyn Patrick

PRACTICAL SELF-CARE STRATEGIES

Imagine a quiet corner of your home transformed into a sanctuary just for you. The soft hum of a lullaby plays in the background, and the gentle aroma of lavender fills the air. This is your space, a haven dedicated to nurturing you through the challenges of motherhood. Creating a postpartum sanctuary is more than just a physical space; it symbolizes a commitment to self-care and mental clarity during this transformative period. In a world where your energy is focused outward, this sanctuary offers a moment to turn inward and recharge, providing a vital sense of peace and renewal.

Designing your sanctuary begins with selecting a calming corner within your home. Choose a spot that feels naturally inviting, perhaps near a window where natural light filters in or in a secluded area where you can retreat undisturbed. The goal is to create a space that welcomes you with open arms, offering comfort and tranquility. Incorporate soothing elements like plush cushions and soft throws to create an inviting atmosphere. Consider adding plants to your space; their presence enhances the aesthetic and promotes a sense of calm, bringing a touch of nature indoors. Soft and adjustable lighting can further enhance the ambiance, allowing you to adjust the mood to suit your needs, whether for relaxation or reflection.

A key aspect of maintaining your sanctuary's serenity is organization. Clutter can cloud the mind and create unnecessary stress. Begin by decluttering the area and removing items that don't contribute to your sense of peace. Storage solutions like baskets or shelves keep essentials neatly organized and within reach. This approach minimizes chaos and ensures that your sanctuary remains a stress-free zone. Maintaining an organized space creates an environment conducive to relaxation and mental clarity, where each item has its place and nothing distracts from the peace you're cultivating.

Sensory elements play a crucial role in enhancing the sanctuary experience. Aromatherapy, using essential oils, can transform the mood and atmosphere of your space. Scents like lavender and chamomile are known for their calming properties, helping to ease tension and promote relaxation. Consider diffusing these oils in your sanctuary, allowing their fragrance to envelop you in a soothing embrace. Accompany the aromatic experience with calming background music or nature sounds. The gentle rustle of leaves or the soft patter of rain can create an auditory landscape that calms the mind and encourages introspection. These sensory elements work together to elevate your sanctuary, making it a true refuge from the demands of daily life.

Protecting your sanctuary time is essential for maintaining its purpose as a space of relaxation and healing. Establish clear boundaries to ensure this time remains uninterrupted. Communicate with your family about the importance of this space and your need for regular solitude. Consider setting "quiet hours" to retreat to your sanctuary without disturbances. This practice reinforces the sanctity of your space and encourages your family to respect your self-care needs. By prioritizing this time, you affirm its importance and integrate it into your routine as a non-negotiable aspect of your well-being.

Reflection Section: Personal Sanctuary Blueprint

Materials Needed:

• Comfortable seating (chair or floor cushion)

• Soft lighting (lamps or fairy-stringed lights)

• Aromatherapy diffuser and essential oils

• Calming music or nature sounds

• Plants (real or artificial)

• Storage solutions (baskets or shelves)

Steps:

1 Choose a quiet corner in your home.

2 Arrange seating and soft lighting.

3 Add plants and organize essentials.

4 Set up aromatherapy and music.

5 Establish "quiet hours" for uninterrupted time.

Taking the time to create and maintain your postpartum sanctuary is an investment in your overall well-being. It's a space that honors your need for rest, reflection, and rejuvenation, providing a touchstone of peace.

Innovative Self-Care Ideas: Tailored for Moms

As you navigate the whirlwind of new motherhood, finding time for self-care can feel like an elusive dream. However, some new innovative self-care ideas are designed specifically for postpartum mothers. Consider the concept of a "mini-retreat," a brief, intentional break that provides a refreshing pause in your day. These retreats could be as simple as savoring a cup of tea while listening to a favorite song or stepping outside to feel the sun on your face. These moments, though short, allow you to recharge and reconnect with yourself. They remind you that you deserve a moment of peace and reflection. Another practice to consider is a "daily gratitude practice." Each day, take a few moments to jot down things you are thankful for. This simple habit can shift your focus from what's overwhelming to what's uplifting, providing mental rejuvenation and grounding.

Incorporating self-care into your daily routine doesn't need to be time-consuming. Think about a five-minute morning meditation to start your day with calm. This practice involves sitting quietly, breathing deeply, and setting a positive intention for the day. It's a powerful way to center yourself before the day's demands take over. Evening reflection journaling offers another opportunity for introspection. Spend a few minutes writing about your day, acknowledging achievements, and releasing any lingering worries. This ritual provides clarity and creates a sense of closure, helping you unwind before sleep. You nurture your mental and emotional well-being in manageable increments by weaving these small self-care activities into your routine.

Technology can be a valuable ally in your self-care journey. Apps like Headspace or Calm offer guided meditations and mindfulness exercises tailored to your needs. They provide a structured way to practice mindfulness, from quick breathing exercises to longer meditations. Online yoga classes can also be a convenient option, allowing you to engage in gentle movement without leaving home. These digital tools make self-care accessible and fit seamlessly into your schedule.

Flexibility is key to making self-care sustainable. Personalize your approach by creating a self-care menu with a variety of options. This menu can include activities ranging from a quick walk in nature to a soothing bath or a few minutes of reading. Rotate these activities based on your mood and energy levels. Some days, you might crave the solitude of a quiet meditation, while other days, a brisk walk might invigorate you. You can tailor your self-care to fit your needs on any given day by having a menu of options. This approach ensures that self-care remains a nourishing practice rather than a chore.

Interactive Element: Self-Care Menu Creation

Materials Needed:

• Your journal or a digital note-taking app

• Inspirational quotes or images (optional)

Steps:

1 List self-care activities that resonate with you.

2 Categorize them by time (e.g., quick, moderate, extended).

3 Incorporate quotes or images for inspiration.

4 Update your menu regularly with new activities.

By embracing these innovative self-care ideas, you create a personalized approach that supports your well-being during the postpartum period. These practices honor your individuality and the unique challenges of motherhood, offering a pathway to enhanced balance and fulfillment.

Stress Relief Techniques: Finding Your Calm

The demands of new motherhood can feel relentless, with stress often lurking beneath the surface. But there are simple and effective techniques that can help you manage stress and find calm. Breathing exercises are a quick way to reduce stress. Imagine taking a deep breath in, feeling your belly expand, and then slowly exhaling, releasing tension with each breath. This simple act helps calm your nervous system and brings immediate relief. Another technique is visualization. Picture yourself in a peaceful setting. A quiet beach, a serene forest, let your mind wander there for a few minutes. Visualization can transport your mind away from the stress, providing a mental escape that refreshes and rejuvenates.

To practice these techniques, first start with guided imagery exercises. Find a comfortable spot, close your eyes, and imagine a place where you feel completely at ease. Focus on the details: the colors, sounds, and sensations. Let yourself be immersed in this vision, letting it wash over you and dissolve stress. Also, try using the progressive muscle relaxation method we discussed earlier. Remember to begin by tensing a specific muscle group, like your shoulders, holding for five seconds, then slowly releasing. Move through different areas of your body, noticing the contrast between tension and relaxation. This practice reduces physical tension and fosters a sense of control over your body's responses to stress.

Regular practice of stress relief techniques is crucial for lasting benefits. The more you engage in these methods, the more effective they become. Consider setting a daily reminder for a stress-relief session that could be as simple as a short break during your day dedicated to mindful breathing or visualization. Using your journal to track your progress can also be insightful. Write down how you feel before and after each session, noting any changes in your stress levels or overall mood. Over time, you'll likely see a pattern of improvement, reinforcing the value of these practices in your daily routine.

Exploring and adapting these techniques to fit your personal needs is key. Experiment with different breathing patterns, such as the 4-7-8 technique, in which you inhale for four counts, hold for seven counts, and then exhale for eight. This technique can deepen relaxation and enhance focus. Tailor visualizations to what resonates with you. It may be a memory from a cherished vacation or an imagined place of tranquility. The goal is to find what works best for you, allowing these practices to integrate seamlessly into your life.

You can discover which ones suit you best by trying different methods. A simple breathing exercise might suffice some days, while a more extended visualization session might be required other times. Personalizing your stress relief routine ensures that it remains effective and enjoyable, providing you with a reliable source of calm.

Me Time: Prioritizing Self Without Guilt

This new realm of motherhood may feel like a delicate dance, balancing your baby's needs, household, and work commitments. Amidst all this, the concept of taking time for yourself may seem indulgent, even selfish. This perception stems from deeply ingrained societal pressures that glorify selflessness in motherhood. The image of the tireless, ever-giving mother is usually celebrated, but this way leaves little room for personal needs. Internalized expectations further reinforce this notion, compelling many mothers to push their desires aside in favor of others. Yet, prioritizing personal time is not an act of self-centeredness but a necessity for preserving your well-being.

Carving out dedicated "me time" in your schedule requires intention and planning. It might seem impossible, but with a few strategies, you can make it happen. Start by scheduling self-care sessions in advance as you would any important meeting. Mark them on your calendar, treating these moments as non-negotiable appointments with yourself. Consider utilizing nap times or early mornings for personal activities. These quiet moments, when the world seems to pause, allow you to focus on yourself without interruptions. Whether reading a book, enjoying a warm bath, or simply sitting in silence, these activities can be a source of rejuvenation. By consciously allotting time for yourself, you affirm the importance of your needs and make self-care a regular part of your routine.

The impact of "me time" extends beyond personal satisfaction; it enriches your overall well-being and parenting. When you prioritize self-care, you nurture a positive mood and replenish your energy reserves, directly enhancing your ability to engage with your family. A well-rested, content parent is more patient and responsive. This practice also models healthy behavior for your children, teaching them the value of self-care and balance. By demonstrating the priority of taking care of oneself, you instill in them the idea that self-care is vital to a balanced life.

A mindset shift is a fundamental part of embracing self-care without guilt. Begin by practicing self-compassion, which involves treating yourself with the same kindness and understanding you would offer a friend. When feelings of guilt arise, counter them with self-affirmations. Remind yourself that you deserve care and attention and that nurturing your well-being benefits those around you. View self-care not as a luxury but as an essential component of health. This perspective shift allows you to approach self-care with openness and acceptance rather than resistance. By reframing self-care as a necessity, you create a foundation of support that empowers you to thrive as a mother.

As you navigate the complexities of motherhood, remember that prioritizing "me time" is a powerful act of self-love. It is an acknowledgment of your worth and a commitment to nurturing the person you are beyond your roles and responsibilities. Embrace these moments as opportunities to reconnect with yourself, knowing that by caring for your needs, you enhance your capacity to care for others.

This chapter has explored practical self-care strategies, emphasizing the importance of creating personal sanctuaries and prioritizing guilt-free self-care. Integrating these practices into your life will nurture you and enhance your capacity to be your best self. As you continue to venture into motherhood, let these strategies guide you toward a path of balance and fulfillment, where self-care becomes an integral part of your daily life. Next, we'll switch our focus to our relationships and the steps required to keep them strong as we grow into our new selves.

RELATIONSHIP DYNAMICS AND GROWTH

It's the end of a long day, and you find yourself on the couch next to your partner, both of you scrolling through your phones in silence. The once vibrant conversations have dwindled, replaced by a quiet routine that feels more like cohabitation than a partnership. This shift into "roommate mode," described by Dr. John Gottman's research, is a common challenge among new parents. It's an adjustment period where the demands of parenthood can overshadow the connection that once came so naturally. The transition to parenthood can strain relationships, with communication often taking a backseat amid the hustle of caring for a newborn. Yet, in these moments, open communication becomes more crucial than ever, serving as the lifeline that can strengthen your partnership and rekindle that sense of unity.

Effective communication is the backbone of any healthy relationship, fostering understanding and intimacy even amid new parenthood turbulence. One of the most powerful tools you can employ is active listening. This means fully focusing on your partner when they speak, setting aside distractions, and truly hearing their words. Nod, maintain eye contact, and reflect back to them what you've understood. This practice not only validates their feelings but also encourages a deeper connection. Regular check-ins with each other are equally important. Set aside time each week, even if it's just 15 minutes, to talk about your experiences, feelings, and any concerns. These moments of connection can prevent misunderstandings and ensure that both partners feel heard and supported.

Initiating difficult conversations with empathy and respect can be challenging, yet it's essential for resolving issues and maintaining harmony. When discussing sensitive topics, "I" statements are your ally. By framing your feelings with "I feel" rather than "You make me feel," you express your emotions without placing blame. For example, "I feel overwhelmed when the housework piles up" opens the door for constructive dialogue. Dedicate specific times for these discussions, choosing moments when both of you are calm and available. This intentionality helps create a safe space for honest communication, reducing the likelihood of conflict and fostering mutual respect.

Empathy, the ability to understand and share the feelings of another, plays a pivotal role in nurturing your relationship during this transformative period. Practicing perspective-taking exercises can enhance this skill. Imagine your partner's day, their challenges, and emotions, and approach your interactions with this understanding. Acknowledge each other's efforts, whether it's the sleepless nights or juggling responsibilities. A simple "Thank you for everything you do" can reaffirm your appreciation and strengthen your bond. When both partners feel seen and valued, it fosters a more profound sense of compassion and connection.

Maintaining emotional intimacy despite the challenges of new parenthood requires creativity and commitment. Small, intentional acts can sustain your emotional connection, even with all the demands of daily life. Sharing daily gratitude notes is one such gesture. Leave a note in their bag or send a text expressing appreciation for something they've done. These small acts can reinforce your emotional bond and remind both of you of the love and support that lives within your relationship. Engaging in activities that promote bonding is equally important. Plan a weekly "date night" at home, where you watch a movie or cook a meal together after the baby is asleep. These shared experiences provide opportunities for laughter and connection, reminding you of the partnership that brought you together in the first place.

When exploring these strategies, remember that every relationship is unique. What works for one couple may not work for another, and that's okay. The key is to find what resonates with you and your partner and adapt these tools to suit your needs. By prioritizing open communication, empathy, and emotional intimacy, you will lay a strong foundation for your relationship and nurture it through the challenges and joys of parenthood.

Reflection Section: Strengthening Your Relationship

Take a few moments to reflect on your current communication patterns. Consider how often you and your partner engage in active listening and regular check-ins. Are there areas where you can improve? Pull out that journal and jot down one or two strategies from this section that you'd like to implement in your relationship. Set a goal to practice these strategies over the next month, and observe any changes in your connection and understanding.

Co-Parenting Strategies: Sharing Responsibilities

The neverending tasks of feeding, diapering, and soothing your baby while coordinating household responsibilities can be overwhelming. Finding balance among all the shared responsibilities becomes crucial. If this balance is mastered, it will strengthen the partnership and enhance your family dynamic. When both parents are equally involved, it fosters a sense of teamwork, which is essential. Co-parenting offers numerous benefits, from improved relationship satisfaction to better outcomes for your child. It allows each parent to bring their strengths to the table, creating a harmonious environment where both parents feel valued and supported. This balanced involvement nurtures a partnership that feels more like a collaboration than a division of labor.

Defining parenting roles can help avoid misunderstandings and conflicts. It's essential to have open discussions about expectations and duties, ensuring that each parent knows their responsibilities. Creating a co-parenting schedule can be a practical tool to facilitate this. It outlines who will handle specific tasks, such as nighttime feedings or grocery shopping, and can be adjusted as needed. For those co-parenting from separate households, this schedule is even more critical. It builds trust and sets clear expectations, ensuring that both parents have a shared understanding of their roles and contributions. This clarity prevents resentment and promotes fairness, which is vital for maintaining a healthy and supportive co-parenting relationship. Mothers who choose to breastfeed exclusively tend to bear a heavy load. Because I chose this path, I achieved balance by giving my spouse most of the diaper duty. The concept of an equal partnership is central to effective co-parenting. It involves ensuring both parents are equally involved in all aspects of parenting. Rotating night shifts or feeding duties can be balanced, allowing both parents to contribute and rest. This reduces the burden on one parent and fosters a sense of shared responsibility.

Effective time management is another key aspect of successful co-parenting. With the demands of parenting and personal needs, prioritizing tasks is crucial. A shared calendar can help track appointments, activities, and responsibilities, ensuring that nothing falls through the cracks. Delegating household chores can also alleviate stress and create more time for family bonding. By sharing these responsibilities, you reduce the pressure on one partner and provide opportunities for both to engage in meaningful interactions with their child.

Establish family rules and routines to create a predictable environment and help your child feel safe. It is also a good idea to address any differing care approaches together and find common ground that aligns with your values and goals. This is especially important when co-parenting from separate homes. Also, try to regularly discuss any feelings of imbalance and apply your active listening skills to prevent misunderstandings and ensure that both parents feel valued.

Once again, appreciation and recognition play a significant role in maintaining a positive co-parenting relationship. Expressing gratitude for specific actions, whether it's preparing a meal or taking the baby for a walk, reinforces the bond between partners. Celebrating successes together, such as your child's first steps or a peaceful bedtime routine, strengthens the connection and fosters a supportive and loving environment. These moments of recognition remind both partners of the shared joy and responsibility they embrace as parents.

Navigating Intimacy: Rediscovering Connection

As you settle into the rhythm of new parenthood, you may find that intimacy with your partner takes on a different shape. The demands of caring for a newborn can leave little room for the spontaneous closeness you once enjoyed. Physical and emotional intimacy often shifts, influenced by the exhaustion that accompanies night feedings and diaper changes. It's common to experience changes in desire as your body is still recovering from childbirth. When it comes to resuming sexual activity, it's crucial to listen to your body and consult with your healthcare provider. Usually, a 4-6 week waiting period is needed before intercourse can resume, and ideally, bleeding should have ceased. Your doctor will also guide you on when it might be safe to resume intimacy, typically after your postpartum check-up. Hormonal changes, such as decreased estrogen, can cause vaginal dryness, adding to the complexity of physical intimacy. Balancing these changes with your intimacy needs requires patience and open communication with your partner.

Rekindling intimacy may need to start with small, intentional steps. Scheduling time together might not sound romantic, but it can be a powerful tool in maintaining your connection. Set aside time when you won't be interrupted, allowing you to focus solely on each other. This doesn't always have to lead to sexual intimacy; sometimes, just being physically close can reignite the bond. Exploring non-physical forms of intimacy can also strengthen your connection. Consider giving each other back rubs, holding hands during a walk, or simply cuddling on the couch. These gestures remind you both of the closeness you share, offering warmth and reassurance amidst the demands of parenthood.

Concerns and insecurities about body image are common after childbirth. Your body has changed, and adjusting to these changes can affect self-esteem and intimacy. It's important to remember that these feelings are normal and shared by many new mothers. Openly discussing your concerns with your partner can be incredibly freeing. Tell them how you feel about your body, and talk about what makes you comfortable or uncomfortable. This dialogue can enhance understanding and create a safe space for intimacy. Communicating desires and boundaries clearly helps both partners feel respected and valued, building trust and confidence in your relationship.

Patience and understanding are vital as you enter this new phase of intimacy. Setting realistic expectations can alleviate pressure and allow you to rediscover your connection at your own pace. Celebrate small moments of connection, whether it's a shared laugh over a silly moment with the baby or a gentle touch in passing. These small gestures build a foundation of intimacy that can grow over time. Remember, every couple's experience is unique, and there's no right or wrong way to reclaim intimacy. Empathy toward each other's experiences fosters a compassionate environment where both partners can express their needs and desires without fear.

Rediscovering connection in the postpartum period is not about returning to what was but rather about creating something new and meaningful. It requires patience, understanding, and a commitment to nurturing your bond. Embrace the changes and find joy in your relationship's evolving landscape.

Conflict Resolution: Addressing Stress Patterns

As the demands of new parenthood settle in, it's not uncommon for tensions to rise. The sleepless nights can wear down even the most patient among us, affecting our moods and ability to communicate effectively. The slightest disagreement can feel monumental when running on just a few hours of uninterrupted sleep. Sleep deprivation isn't just about physical fatigue; it impacts your emotional resilience, making it harder to navigate the complexities of a relationship. Financial stress adds another layer of pressure. The shift from two incomes to one, or the added expenses a new baby brings, can spark anxiety and disagreements about budgeting. These stressors create a fertile ground for conflict, underscoring the need for effective conflict resolution strategies.

When disagreements arise, approaching them with a resolution mindset rather than opposition can make all the difference. One technique that can be remarkably effective is the use of time-outs. When a discussion escalates, taking a moment to step back allows both partners to cool down before continuing. This pause can prevent hurtful words from being said in the heat of the moment. During this time, focus on calming your mind through deep breathing or a quick walk. Once emotions have settled, you can return to the conversation with a clearer perspective. Practicing conflict resolution dialogues is another powerful tool. This struc-tured communication involves each partner taking turns to speak and listen, ensuring both voices are heard. By focusing on under-standing rather than winning, couples can resolve conflicts more constructively.

Despite your best efforts, there may be times when conflicts persist and external support becomes necessary. Seeking guidance from professionals, such as couples therapists or counselors, can offer a fresh perspective and equip you with new strategies for resolving disagreements. These experts can help identify underlying issues that might be contributing to recurring conflicts, offering tailored advice and support. Parenting workshops and support groups also provide valuable opportunities to connect with others facing similar challenges. Sharing experiences and learning from others can reduce feelings of isolation, providing reassurance that you're not alone.

Forgiveness is crucial to conflict resolution, allowing couples to move forward without the burden of past grievances. Holding onto grudges can hinder growth and create distance in a relationship. Instead, try practicing forgiveness exercises in order to facilitate healing and reconnection. Start by acknowledging your partner's perspective and expressing a willingness to let go of resentment. This doesn't mean ignoring the issue but instead prioritizing the relationship over the conflict. Re-establishing trust and communication is vital after a disagreement. Take time to reaffirm your commitment to each other, highlighting the strengths and values that unite you. This process creates a sense of togetherness, reinforcing the idea that you are a team capable of overcoming challenges.

When tackling these stress patterns and conflicts, remember that you and your partner are on the same side. Approach each disagreement with empathy, seeking solutions that honor both perspectives. It's not about avoiding conflict but managing it in a way that strengthens your relationship. By embracing these strategies, you can create a more harmonious and supportive partnership, paving the way for a loving and nurturing family environment.

Family dynamics and life circumstances are incredibly diverse, making it impossible to address every scenario in a single book. However, I've discovered some common threads through countless conversations with other moms. Becoming a mother means stepping into a world shaped by timeless traditions and ever-evolving expectations. But there's a path to balancing family advice, cultural practices, and your unique choices. In the next chapter, we'll explore how to confidently navigate these other dynamics, blending the past and present to craft your motherhood experience.

EXPLORING THE TRADITIONAL AND NONTRADITIONAL ASPECTS OF NEW MOTHERHOOD

I magine a bustling family gathering where everyone has an opinion on how to care for your newborn. Your mother-in-law offers what she calls "timeless wisdom" while your siblings debate the best sleep schedules. As a new mother, you might find yourself forging through a complex maze of family dynamics and well-meaning advice. The arrival of a baby can bring joy, but it also shifts established relationships, creating new challenges. Taking in and analyzing all the different cultural or generational perspectives as you adjust to your new role can be overwhelming.

In-law relationships, in particular, can present unique challenges. While they might offer invaluable support and experience, they can also bring expectations that clash with your parenting style. It's common to feel caught between wanting to honor their advice and asserting your approach. Addressing these cultural or generational differences requires open dialogue and understanding. It's important to acknowledge their intentions while gently expressing your own needs and preferences. This can help create a harmonious environment where everyone feels valued and respected.

Setting clear boundaries with family members becomes essential in this context. It's about communicating your needs and limits effectively. Try using "I" statements during these instances. Instead of saying, "You're overwhelming me with advice," try, "I appreciate your help, but I need space to find my own way." This approach reduces defensiveness and encourages constructive conversations. Setting limits on visitations and unsolicited advice is equally important. You might say, "We'd love to have visitors, but we need some quiet time as a family today." These boundaries ensure that your family's needs are prioritized and respected, reducing potential conflicts and fostering a supportive atmosphere.

Balancing support and independence can also be a delicate dance. Accepting help without guilt can be challenging, especially when it feels like you should be able to manage everything on your own. However, it's essential to recognize that receiving support doesn't diminish your capabilities. It's a testament to your strength and wisdom.

Family conflicts are inevitable but can be resolved constructively with the right strategies. Mediation techniques can be highly effective in diffusing tension. Consider inviting a neutral third party to facilitate discussions, ensuring everyone feels heard and respected. They can guide you through actively listening to each other's perspectives and acknowledging your differing viewpoints. It's about finding common ground and working together to create solutions that benefit everyone involved.

Reflection Exercise: Setting Boundaries with Confidence

Take a moment to reflect on the boundaries you'd like to establish with your family. Consider the areas where you need more support or space. Write down your needs and practice using "I" statements to express them. Role-playing these conversations with a partner can build confidence and prepare you for real-life discussions. Remember, setting boundaries is an act of self-care and a way to prioritize your well-being. By clearly communicating your needs, you create an environment that supports your family's growth and happiness.

The Postpartum Single Parent

You may find yourself in the quiet hours of the night, holding your newborn, feeling both the weight and wonder of single parenthood. While filled with unique challenges, this path also brings its own strengths. You're navigating the postpartum period without a partner, which requires resilience and resourcefulness. Physical and emotional recovery may feel demanding as you manage healing while caring for a newborn. It's crucial to prioritize your well-being to support your role as the sole caregiver. Establishing a routine becomes your lifeline. It offers predictability in a world that feels anything but predictable. Creating a schedule that balances your baby's needs with your own allows for moments of rest and self-care. Remember, a routine doesn't have to be rigid; it's about finding a flow that works for you and your child. This structure will lead to a sense of stability and control.

Balancing self-care and newborn care is a delicate act. It's easy to fall into the trap of putting your needs last, but remember that a well-cared-for parent is better equipped to care for their child. Small moments of self-care—like a warm bath, a quiet cup of tea, or even a few deep breaths—can recharge you. Accept help from friends, family, or community resources without guilt. It takes a village, and reaching out for support is a sign of strength. Practical tips can make baby care more manageable. Consider babywearing to keep your little one close while having your hands free for daily tasks. Preparing meals in advance or opting for easy, nutritious snacks can save time and energy. Prioritize tasks and let go of non-essential chores. Simplifying your environment and routines can reduce stress and create more space for bonding with your baby.

Being a sole provider and caregiver comes with its own set of challenges. You may find yourself juggling work, finances, and parenting, each demanding your full attention. Navigating these responsibilities requires creativity and planning. If you're returning to work, explore flexible or remote work options that accommodate your parenting needs. Communicate with your employer about your situation, and don't hesitate to ask for support or accommodations. Managing important tasks while caring for your baby can feel overwhelming, but breaking them into smaller, manageable steps can make a difference. Use lists to prioritize tasks and set realistic goals for each day. Embrace technology that can help streamline tasks, like grocery delivery services or online scheduling tools.

Balancing parenting with work and other responsibilities may feel like a constant tightrope walk. Yet, within this balance lies the opportunity to discover your resilience and adaptability. The strength you cultivate during these moments serves as a foundation for the life you're building with your child. Embrace the uniqueness of your journey, knowing that you are crafting a home filled with love, determination, and a deep sense of accomplishment.

Postpartum Management of Pets and Furry Companions

As you prepare to welcome your newborn, your furry companion might sense the changes afoot. Pets, much like us, thrive on routine and predictability. Introducing them to a new baby requires thoughtfulness and preparation to ensure a harmonious household. Begin by gradually acclimating your pet to the concept of a baby. Play recordings of baby sounds at varying volumes to desensitize your pet to these new noises. Rearrange furniture slowly, allowing them to explore new setups like the nursery. This helps them adjust without feeling overwhelmed by sudden changes. Creating safe spaces for both your pet and baby is crucial. Designate a quiet area for your pet to retreat when they need calm. For your baby, ensure that their sleeping and play areas are free from pet access, preventing any accidental mishaps. Recognizing signs of stress or anxiety in your pet, such as excessive barking or hiding, can guide you in providing comfort and reassurance.

Introducing your pet to the baby should be a gradual process. Allow your pet to observe from a distance initially, rewarding calm behavior with treats and praise. Over time, let them approach under supervision. This builds trust and curiosity in a controlled manner. Finding time to bond with your pet and baby might seem daunting, but it's vital for maintaining your pet's well-being. Consider incorporating your pet into daily routines. A walk with the stroller benefits both baby and pet, providing exercise and fresh air. Let your pet sit nearby during feeding or playtime, fostering a sense of inclusion without direct interaction. Managing jealousy or territorial behavior requires patience. Reinforce positive interactions and ignore negative ones, ensuring your pet feels secure in their place within the family. Anxiety can often be addressed through increased play and attention, reinforcing their importance in your life.

Including your pet in daily activities strengthens their bond with the family. If your pet is accustomed to bedtime cuddles, maintain this ritual, perhaps with your baby in a safe nearby bassinet. Pets often mirror our emotions, so maintaining a calm demeanor helps them adjust to new routines. Set aside dedicated time to engage with your pet through play, grooming, or training sessions. This reassures them that they're still a cherished member of the household. Introducing new commands or reinforcing existing ones can boost their confidence and reduce anxiety. Remember, your pet's world has changed, too, and with patience and understanding, they can become a loving and loyal companion to your child.

Global Postpartum Practices: Insights and Adaptations

In many cultures around the world, the postpartum period is a time steeped in tradition and care, with practices that have been passed down through generations. In China, the tradition of "zuo yue zi," or "sitting the month," involves a period of rest and recuperation following childbirth. During this time, mothers are encouraged to rest, avoid physical exertion, and consume specific foods believed to aid recovery and milk production. This practice highlights the importance of healing the body before resuming daily activities. Similarly, in India, postpartum confinement practices emphasize rest, dietary restrictions, and herbal baths. These traditions are designed to protect the new mother and help her regain strength. In various African cultures, community support systems, often involving doulas, play a crucial role. These women provide physical and emotional support, assisting with baby care and household tasks, allowing new mothers to focus on bonding with their newborns and recovering.

These global practices share a common goal: to support postpartum recovery and strengthen the bond between mother and child. Rest is emphasized, recognizing that the postpartum body requires time to heal. Nutritional support is also a cornerstone, with traditional diets rich in nourishing soups and herbs that promote healing and lactation. These practices are not just about physical recovery but also about fostering emotional well-being. By providing a supportive environment, they allow new mothers to transition into their roles with confidence and ease. This focus on community and care helps mitigate the feelings of isolation that can accompany new motherhood, reinforcing the notion that it truly takes a village to raise a child.

Adapting these beneficial practices to modern lifestyles can enhance your postpartum experience. Consider incorporating rest periods into your day, even if it's just a few minutes of quiet time. Embrace the idea of nourishment through food, exploring recipes for soups and stews that are both comforting and nutritious. Introducing elements of these traditions can provide a sense of grounding and connection, even in a busy modern life. However, it's essential to balance tradition with personal comfort. Not every practice may resonate with you, and that's okay. Choose what feels right for you and your family, adapting as needed to fit your lifestyle and preferences.

Integrating these practices into contemporary settings may present challenges. Family expectations and cultural pressures can complicate the process, especially if your choices differ from traditional norms. It's vital to clearly communicate your needs and boundaries, explaining your choices and the reasons behind them. Balancing tradition with modern life requires flexibility and understanding. You might face resistance, but remember that your comfort and well-being are paramount. Navigating these complexities involves honoring your heritage while embracing new ways that align with your values and circumstances.

Celebrating Diversity: Embracing Different Traditions

Imagine a room filled with laughter and stories where each person shares a piece of their heritage. Embracing cultural diversity in parenting enriches the experience, bringing a tapestry of traditions and wisdom. Each culture offers unique perspectives, adding depth and richness to the parenting mosaic. Recognizing the value of these varied cultural perspectives helps us appreciate the different ways families across the globe celebrate life and nurture their children. This appreciation not only broadens our understanding but also encourages a deeper connection with our cultural roots, fostering a sense of pride and belonging.

In African cultures, naming ceremonies are significant events that go beyond simply choosing a name. These ceremonies often involve the entire community, celebrating the child's place within the extended family and culture. Similarly, Native American traditions like Blessingways offer a spiritual celebration for the mother-to-be, focusing on her transition into motherhood. These traditions highlight the communal aspect of childbirth and parenting, underscoring the belief that raising a child is a collective endeavor. Such practices remind us of the importance of community support and shared joy in the parenting process.

Embracing diversity enriches the parenting experience by opening doors to learning from various cultural backgrounds. Participating in multicultural parenting groups can provide insights and support, offering a platform to exchange cultural practices. These groups create an inclusive space where diverse parenting styles are celebrated, and mutual respect is established. Sharing cultural practices encourages understanding and empathy, building bridges between different communities. Culturally tailored educational materials can also provide valuable resources, offering guidance that respects and incorporates cultural nuances. This exchange of knowledge and traditions enhances the parenting journey, creating a more inclusive and supportive family environment.

Modern Motherhood: Balancing Tradition and Innovation

Picture a modern mother juggling conference calls, baby feedings, and a moment of meditation, all before noon. The landscape of motherhood today is vastly different from that of past generations, presenting unique challenges as you aim to balance traditional postpartum practices with the demands of contemporary life. Navigating career and family life is a significant hurdle. Many mothers find themselves returning to work sooner than anticipated, driven by economic necessity or career aspirations. This shift demands a delicate balance as you strive to maintain professional commitments while nurturing your newborn. Urban settings further complicate access to traditional support systems, often leaving you without the nearby family networks that once provided essential postpartum care.

In this context, innovative approaches to postpartum care become invaluable. Online communities and support groups offer a lifeline, connecting you with other mothers who share similar experiences. These platforms provide a space to exchange advice, share stories, and offer support, all from the comfort of your home. Similarly, technology has revolutionized postpartum education, with apps and online courses offering guidance on everything from breastfeeding techniques to managing postpartum depression. These resources empower you to integrate traditional wisdom with modern knowledge, creating a holistic approach to postpartum care.

Preserving cultural heritage amid modern advancements is a balancing act. It involves passing down traditional practices while embracing the conveniences of contemporary life. For example, you might combine ancestral remedies with modern healthcare, creating a personalized approach that honors your heritage. Sharing stories and rituals with your child fosters a sense of connection to their roots, even as you adapt to the demands of modern living. This fusion of old and new enriches your family's narrative, ensuring that cultural traditions remain vibrant and relevant in today's world.

Crafting a personalized postpartum plan allows you to navigate these complexities with intention. A flexible plan respects cultural traditions while accommodating your unique circumstances. Consider incorporating meaningful family rituals into your daily routine through meals, music, or storytelling. These acts create continuity and connection, grounding you in your cultural identity. At the same time, embrace modern practices that support your wellbeing, such as postpartum yoga or digital mental health resources. This blend of tradition and innovation ensures that your postpartum experience is well-rounded.

As you forge your path through modern motherhood, remember you are not alone. Countless mothers are navigating similar challenges, each crafting their own blend of tradition and innovation. Your journey is a testament to resilience and adaptability, a dance between honoring the past and embracing the future. While the road may be complex, the rewards are profound: a thriving family rooted in heritage yet open to the possibilities of modern life. Now, let's delve into the dynamics of returning to work and balancing life as a new mother.

RETURNING TO WORK AND BALANCING LIFE

R eturning to work after having a baby can be a rollercoaster of emotions, much like standing on the edge of a diving board, peering into the pool below. The anticipation is palpable, tinged with excitement and a hint of fear about the unknown depth. As a new mother, you might find yourself torn between the eagerness to return to a semblance of your pre-baby life and the guilt of leaving your little one behind. Many mothers grapple with this duality, where the heartstrings pull one way while the mind urges another. The conflict encompasses the emotional and practical aspects of re-entering the workforce. The joy of engaging with colleagues and the satisfaction of work can coexist with the pang of separation anxiety. This chapter is designed to help you navigate these mixed emotions while equipping you with the tools to manage the logistics of this transition.

One of the first steps in easing this transition is planning for child-care. It's crucial to start early, as finding the right arrangement can take time, and having a trusted caregiver in place can significantly alleviate anxiety. Whether you opt for a daycare, a nanny, or family help, each choice has nuances and requires thoughtful consideration.

Visit potential daycare centers, interview nannies, or have candid conversations with family members about expectations and schedules. This groundwork ensures your child is in safe hands and provides peace of mind, knowing they are cared for in your absence. Balancing work and motherhood is a dance; having a reliable support system is like having a strong partner to guide you through the steps.

As you return to work, scheduling a meeting with your HR department is vital. Discuss your maternity leave options and inquire about any available phased return programs. Many organizations offer the flexibility to gradually increase work hours, easing you back into the routine without the shock of a full-time schedule from day one. These discussions can also cover potential adjustments, such as remote work or altered hours, that might better suit your new lifestyle. A phased approach allows you to acclimate at a pace that respects your needs and your baby's. It's about finding a rhythm that works for you, allowing for a smoother transition that honors your professional and personal responsibilities.

Open communication with your employer is key to setting clear expectations. Proactively discussing flexible work arrangements can pave the way for a supportive work environment. Whether negotiating a work-from-home day, adjusting start and end times, or even setting up regular check-ins with supervisors, these conversations help create a framework that accommodates your new role as a mother. Flexibility is a valuable asset, and fostering a dialogue with your employer ensures you have the support you need to thrive at work and at home. Regular check-ins with your supervisor provide opportunities to reassess your workload and make necessary adjustments, ensuring that your transition back to work is as seamless as possible.

Maintaining a work-life balance in this new chapter involves meticulous planning and prioritization. Creating a clear to-do list can help you manage tasks effectively, ensuring you focus on high-priority items without feeling overwhelmed. Block scheduling, where you group similar tasks together, can enhance efficiency and free up time for family and self-care. It's also important to allocate specific times for work and family, creating boundaries that allow you to be present and engaged in each role. This might mean setting aside an hour each evening for uninterrupted family time or designating a weekend morning for personal activities. Finding this balance is a dynamic process, and it may require regular adjustments as you navigate the demands of work and motherhood.

Interactive Element: Creating a Transition Plan

Consider creating a personalized transition plan to support your journey back to work. This plan can outline your childcare arrangements, work schedule adjustments, and communication strategies with your employer. Use a simple table or chart to map out key dates, contact information, and actionable steps. This visual roadmap can serve as a reassuring guide, helping you confidently manage the logistical and emotional aspects of returning to work. Remember, this plan is flexible and can be adapted as your needs and circumstances evolve.

As you embark on this new phase, remember that feeling a mix of emotions is okay. Excitement about returning to work can coexist with the sadness of leaving your baby. These feelings are valid, and acknowledging them is part of the process. Be kind to yourself, and give yourself grace as you find your footing. You can transition back to work with proper preparation and support while maintaining a fulfilling and balanced life.

Pumping at Work: Making it Manageable

Navigating the logistics of pumping at work can initially seem overwhelming. However, understanding your rights and workplace policies can transform this challenge into a manageable routine. Under the Fair Labor Standards Act (FLSA), many employers are required to provide nursing mothers with reasonable break time and a private space (other than a bathroom) to pump breast milk for up to a year after childbirth. Knowing these rights empowers you to advocate for the support you need. It's vital to familiarize yourself with your workplace's specific lactation policies. Some companies have designated lactation rooms, while others may allow you to use a private office space. If your workplace lacks a clear policy, consider discussing your needs with human resources to ensure a comfortable and supportive environment.

Setting up a pumping routine at work requires some advance planning. Begin by scheduling regular pumping breaks that align with your baby's feeding schedule. The consistency of these breaks is crucial for maintaining milk supply, so try to plan them at the same times each day. It might be helpful to block these times on your calendar to avoid scheduling conflicts. Creating a discrete and comfortable pumping space is equally important. If your workplace provides a lactation room, take the time to familiarize yourself with the space before your first day back. Ensure it meets your privacy, cleanliness, and comfort needs. If such a space is unavailable, consider using a portable, collapsible screen to create privacy in an unused conference room or office. Having a comfortable chair and a small table within arm's reach can make the process more pleasant.

Organization and preparation are your allies in making pumping manageable. Packing a portable cooler bag for milk storage is a simple yet effective strategy. An insulated bag with ice packs can keep your milk safe until you're ready to head home. It's also wise to keep spare parts and cleaning supplies at work. Consider storing an extra set of pump flanges, valves, and membranes in your desk drawer or locker. A small bag with cleaning wipes and a hand towel can be handy for quick clean-ups between sessions. I found a small collapsable bowl for cleaning parts to be very convenient.

My favorite hack was storing flanges from my first pumping session in a freezer bag and then putting them in the fridge to prevent bacterial growth, just in case I was on a time crunch and couldn't clean between sessions. Being prepared minimizes stress and ensures you're always ready to pump, even if a piece of equipment is accidentally left at home. TRUST ME, it will happen. To avoid the dreaded act of leaving the milk at work, set an alarm or put a sticky note on your car's dashboard. Mine simply wrote, "GOT MILK?" Oh, another reminder to put the milk in the fridge when you get home is just as important! I can't tell you how many tears I shed from getting distracted and forgetting to put the milk in the refrigerator. If at all possible, have a breast milk stash; I wish I had more of a stash back then to cover me for all those forgetful times. But please do not stress if you are unable to produce one; my baby was just fine with what I did have.

Communicating all your needs with your employer and colleagues is also important. Discussing your pumping schedule with management can help set expectations and prevent interruptions during your breaks. You might find it helpful to explain the importance of these sessions for both your baby's health and your own comfort. Educating colleagues about the necessity of pumping can also promote a more supportive workplace culture. While it's a personal choice how much you wish to share, a simple explanation can garner their understanding and respect.

If you encounter any resistance or challenges, remember that many resources are available to support you. The Department of Labor provides information on your rights, and organizations like La Leche League offer resources and support groups for breastfeeding mothers. These networks can provide guidance and encouragement, reminding you that you're not alone in balancing work and breastfeeding. Knowing your rights and preparing for the logistics of pumping can make the process smoother and more manageable, allowing you to focus on what truly matters: providing for your baby while maintaining your professional responsibilities.

Time Management: Juggling Responsibilities

Balancing the myriad roles of work, family, and personal time can feel like a complex puzzle, with each piece demanding your attention simultaneously. As a working mother, you face the challenge of effectively managing your time while ensuring that no aspect of your life is neglected. The hustle and bustle of daily routines can often lead to time-wasting activities that don't add value to your day. Recognizing these distractions is the first step towards reclaiming your time. Consider the minutes lost scrolling through social media or the hours spent on tasks that could be streamlined. Identifying these culprits lets you focus your energy on what truly matters, helping you craft a more efficient schedule that aligns with your priorities.

Delegation is another powerful tool for managing time effectively. As a mother, it's natural to feel like you should handle everything yourself, but accepting help can lighten your load significantly. Recognize the tasks that can be passed on to others, whether asking a family member to help with school drop-offs or enlisting a partner's assistance with household chores. Delegating doesn't mean relinquishing control; it's about sharing responsibilities to create a harmonious environment where everyone contributes. This frees up your time and fosters a sense of teamwork and support within your household. By acknowledging that you don't have to do it all, you open the door to a more balanced life where each family member plays a part.

Incorporating practical time management strategies into your routine can optimize productivity and balance. Digital planners and apps can serve as invaluable allies in organizing your day. They offer a centralized hub for scheduling appointments, setting reminders, and tracking tasks. Utilize these tools to create a structured plan that outlines your daily, weekly, and monthly goals. Create a family calendar to track activities and commitments, ensuring everyone is on the same page. This visual tool can help coordinate schedules, prevent conflicts, and allow smoother transitions between work, family, and personal time.

Setting priorities is key; focus on what's urgent and important, leaving less critical tasks for later. This prioritization helps you maintain clarity and purpose, ensuring that each day is spent productively. When setting goals, be realistic about what you can achieve in a given timeframe. Overloading your schedule can lead to stress and burnout, counteracting the benefits of an organized plan.

Self-care is an integral part of effective time management. With all the responsibilities looming, carving out time for yourself is crucial. I cannot stress this enough: scheduling regular breaks for relaxation will rejuvenate your mind and body, helping you recharge and maintain focus. Whether it's a few quiet moments with a cup of tea or a short walk outside, these breaks offer respite from the daily grind. Incorporate self-care into your daily routine by setting aside time for activities that nurture you, such as reading, meditating, or exercising. These moments of self-care are not indulgent; they are necessary for sustaining the energy needed for all your multifaceted roles.

In managing your time as a working mother, it's important to remember that perfection is not the goal. Balancing work, family, and personal life is an ongoing process that requires flexibility and adaptability. There will be days when everything falls into place and others when chaos reigns. Simply embrace these fluctuations and give yourself grace.

Setting Boundaries: Protecting Your Time and Energy

In life, your time will always feel like a precious commodity. Setting boundaries is the key to balancing the demands of work and motherhood. Boundaries are like invisible fences that protect your personal time and energy from being consumed by external demands. They help you define where work ends and personal life begins, ensuring that neither encroaches upon the other. Establishing "no work" zones and times is a practical way to create these boundaries. This might mean designating certain hours in the evening or weekends as strictly family time, during which work emails remain unchecked and your focus remains on loved ones. These deliberate separations create a mental and emotional buffer, allowing you to be fully present in whatever you're doing, whether it's a meeting at work or a bedtime story at home.

Communicating boundaries clearly to colleagues and family is crucial for their effectiveness. Your colleagues need to understand when you're available for work-related matters and when you're not. Be upfront about your working hours and any specific times when you're not to be disturbed. This transparency helps manage expectations and reduces the likelihood of work creeping into your personal time. Similarly, your family should know when you need uninterrupted time for work or personal projects. These conversations might initially feel awkward, but they pave the way for mutual respect and understanding. This clarity empowers you to prioritize your well-being, ensuring that both work and family get the attention they deserve.

To enforce boundaries effectively, adopt assertive communication techniques. Assertiveness involves expressing your needs and limits confidently and respectfully. Practice saying "no" to non-essential tasks that threaten to overwhelm your schedule. This doesn't mean declining every request but rather discerning which tasks align with your priorities and which do not. Doing so preserves your time and energy for what truly matters. This approach creates a sense of control over your commitments, reducing the stress and burnout that can arise from overextending yourself. Remember, it's not selfish to protect your time; it's a necessary step in maintaining your health and happiness.

Regular reevaluation and adjustment of boundaries are essential as circumstances change. Life is dynamic, and your needs and priorities will evolve over time. Periodically review your boundaries to ensure they still serve you well. Are there new challenges that require different limits? Have your responsibilities shifted, necessitating an adjustment in how you allocate your time? Being flexible with your boundaries allows you to respond to life's changes adequately. It's about finding a balance that reflects your current situation, ensuring that your boundaries remain a source of support rather than a constraint.

As we wrap up this chapter on returning to work and balancing life, the importance of setting and maintaining boundaries becomes clear. They are not just rules to follow but tools to enhance your quality of life by protecting your time and energy. The next chapter will explore the lifelong wellness habits that will sustain you through motherhood and beyond.

LIFELONG WELLNESS AND EMPOWERMENT

The sun peeks through the curtains, casting a gentle warmth over the room as you stir from sleep. The day is new, and with it comes the opportunity to nurture your baby and yourself. The postpartum period is an ideal time to establish wellness habits that will serve you long after the immediate demands of new motherhood have passed. Developing a balanced routine that includes physical activity and rest lays the groundwork for a healthier, more fulfilling life. Exercise rejuvenates the body and mind, providing energy and clarity, while rest allows your body to recover and rejuvenate. Integrating these practices into your daily life helps you maintain vitality, which is essential not just for motherhood but for every role you play.

Prioritizing mental health alongside physical health is crucial. The demands of motherhood can easily overshadow your emotional needs, yet nurturing your mental well-being is just as important as caring for your body. Consider setting aside a few moments each day for the mindfulness practices we discussed. Meditation and deep breathing can ground you and reduce stress. Regularly engaging in activities that bring you joy, whether it's reading, painting, or gardening, can also elevate your mood and provide a sense of fulfillment. Balancing your mental and physical health creates a harmonious foundation supporting you through life's transitions.

As life evolves, maintaining wellness habits requires adaptability. Setting achievable goals is key. Start small and build gradually. You may begin by committing to a 10-minute walk each day or incorporating one meatless meal into your weekly menu. Adjust your goals to match your progress and needs as you grow more comfortable. Involving your family in these activities can make the process enjoyable and sustainable. Remember, family, walks, cooking nutritious meals together, or even sharing a yoga session can reinforce bonds while promoting health. By embedding wellness into family life, you create a supportive environment that encourages everyone to thrive.

Preventive health measures play an essential role in lifelong wellness. Regular health screenings and check-ups allow you to monitor your health and catch potential issues early. Schedule these appointments as you would any important meeting, prioritizing them as part of your self-care routine. Remember, your well-being is a top priority, and preventive measures are tools that safeguard your future health.

Embracing a diet rich in fruits, vegetables, whole grains, and legumes provides essential nutrients and supports your health. It's not about strict adherence but instead making small incorporations where you, eventually, a diverse and nourishing diet will arrive.

Interactive Element: Reflection and Goal-Setting Exercise

Take a moment to reflect on your current wellness habits. Consider what you do well and areas for improvement. Write down three wellness goals you want to achieve in the next six months. Reflect on how these goals align with your values and how they can enhance your life. Keep this list visible as a reminder of your commitment to your well-being.

By embracing these wellness habits, you invest in a future where health and vitality are within reach. Nurturing your body and mind enhances your quality of life and sets a powerful example for your family.

Embracing Change: Continuous Growth and Learning

Change is an inevitable part of life, constantly shaping and reshaping our experiences. It can feel overwhelming, especially when entering into this new terrain of motherhood, but viewing change as an opportunity rather than a challenge opens doors to personal growth. Embracing change allows you to develop new skills, gain fresh perspectives, and uncover hidden strengths. Each stage of transformation, from initial discomfort to eventual acceptance, holds valuable lessons. This process is akin to a caterpillar becoming a butterfly; though the journey may be arduous, the outcome is a beautiful testament to your ability to adapt. By welcoming change, you allow yourself to evolve and thrive, finding new facets of your identity along the way.

Adapting to change requires flexibility and a willingness to step outside your comfort zone. Practicing adaptability involves being open to new ideas and approaches, even when they differ from what you know. This skill is invaluable in motherhood, where each day brings unexpected challenges and joys. Consider the analogy of a tree bending in the wind; it withstands the storm by being flexible yet rooted. By embracing the unexpected, you empower yourself to face whatever comes your way with confidence and poise.

Affirmations can help cultivate a positive mindset, reinforcing one's belief in one's ability to grow and succeed. Simple affirmations like "I am capable" or "I embrace change with courage" can transform one's mindset, boosting confidence and motivation.

Empowerment Through Knowledge: Staying Informed

Knowledge is a powerful tool that can uplift and empower you, especially during the transformative phase of motherhood. By staying informed, you can confidently make decisions pertaining to your health, your child's development, or family dynamics. Accessing reliable sources of information is crucial. Seek out well-respected publications, scientific studies, and expert advice that provide factual and unbiased insights. Engaging in informed discussions with healthcare providers further enhances your decision-making process. It allows you to ask pertinent questions, clarify doubts, and ensure that your choices are well-aligned with your values and the best interests of your family.

Keeping current with health, parenting, and wellness developments requires intentional effort. Subscribing to reputable newsletters and journals can be a convenient way to receive updates and insights directly to your inbox. These resources often offer summaries of the latest research, practical tips, and expert opinions that can be invaluable in your journey. I can't say I read every email, but every once in a while, a topic will pique my interest and teach me something new. Online forums and discussion groups also provide a platform for sharing experiences and learning from others. Engaging in these virtual communities can connect you with parents who are having similar challenges, offering both support and new perspectives. However, it's essential to approach these spaces with discernment, recognizing that not all information shared online is accurate or applicable to your situation.

Critical thinking and discernment are key when consuming information. In an age where misinformation can spread rapidly, evaluating the credibility of sources is essential. Be mindful of identifying bias and misinformation, which can skew your understanding and lead to misinformed decisions. Comparing multiple perspectives on a topic can help you gain a well-rounded view, allowing you to weigh the pros and cons before making decisions. This vigilant approach to information consumption ensures that your choices are grounded in reality and reflect the diverse viewpoints available. It also enhances your ability to advocate for yourself and your family, equipping you with the knowledge to question, explore, and understand complex issues.

Resource List: Trusted Information Sources

• PubMed: A resource for accessing a wide range of scientific studies and medical research.

• The American College of Obstetricians and Gynecologists (ACOG): Offers guidelines and updates on women's health and postpartum care.

• La Leche League International: Provides support and information on breastfeeding and parenting.

• Parenting Science: A website that explores the science behind parenting practices and child development.

Being informed is not just about acquiring knowledge but about using it to make empowered choices. By staying informed, engaging with others, and approaching information critically, you equip yourself with the tools needed to thrive in motherhood. This proactive approach fosters confidence, resilience, and a deeper understanding of the world around you.

Celebrating Your Journey: Reflection and Gratitude

In the whirlwind of daily life, it's easy to overlook your own growth. However, taking time to reflect on personal progress is vital. I can't say it enough! Pull out that journal; it's a tangible record of your thoughts, challenges, and triumphs. This practice lets you see how far you've come, acknowledging the milestones that mark your journey as a new mother. Each entry, whether it details a sleepless night conquered or a tender moment shared with your child, becomes a testament to your resilience. Celebrating these achievements with family and friends can further reinforce your sense of accomplishment. Sharing these moments not only strengthens bonds but also provides a support network that appreciates your unique experiences.

And don't forget the gratitude! It's a powerful tool that can transform your perspective, creating a mindset of appreciation and contentment. Writing daily gratitude lists can help you focus on the positive aspects of your life, shifting attention from stressors to blessings. This simple act encourages you to notice the small, often overlooked joys that fill your days. Expressing appreciation to those around you deepens relationships and builds a community rooted in kindness and understanding. Whether it's a heartfelt thank you to a partner who took on an extra task or a note to a friend who listened, these gestures nurture connections that support you through motherhood's challenges.

The benefits of reflection and gratitude extend beyond immediate happiness, contributing significantly to mental health. Engaging in these practices can reduce stress, enhance positive emotions, and build emotional resilience. When you focus on what's good in your life, you create a buffer against anxiety and negativity. This shift in perspective can lead to stronger, more fulfilling relationships. In essence, gratitude acts as a bridge, connecting you to others and reinforcing the support network that fortifies you during difficult times.

Setting future goals and aspirations can infuse your days with optimism and purpose. Creating a vision board filled with images and words that resonate with your dreams can be a daily reminder of what you aspire to achieve. This visual representation of your goals keeps them tangible and within reach. Setting intentions for continued growth and fulfillment helps you focus on what truly matters. These aspirations guide your actions, ensuring you remain aligned with your values and passions as you evolve as a mother.

As you celebrate your journey, embrace the growth and change that come with it. Acknowledge your achievements, practice gratitude, and set meaningful goals for the future. This chapter of your life offers immense opportunities for reflection, learning, and connection. By cultivating all the practices you've learned in this book, you enhance your well-being and enrich the lives of those around you.

CONCLUSION

As we close this book, let's take a moment to reflect on the journey we've traveled together through the fourth trimester. While challenging, this period is also a time of profound transformation and growth. We've explored a wide range of topics, from the physical recovery after childbirth to the emotional adjustments new mothers face. Each chapter was designed to equip you with the knowledge and strategies needed to take on this unique phase of your life with confidence and grace.

Throughout this book, we've highlighted the importance of proactive postpartum care. By understanding the physical and emotional changes that occur during the fourth trimester, you can better prepare yourself for the road ahead. Remember, prioritizing your mental health is just as crucial as caring for your newborn.

I encourage you to actively engage with the advice and exercises shared in this book. Each section is a resource you can revisit whenever you need a boost or a reminder of the strategies that resonate with you. The supportive community resources we've discussed are there to offer additional guidance and connection. You're not alone on this journey; countless others have walked the same path and are willing to support you.

Your new role as a mother comes with its own set of challenges. However, with the empowerment gained through your new knowledge and self-awareness, you have the power to overcome anything this trimester throws at you. I believe in you, mama; I know you've got this!

Thank you for allowing me to be a part of your journey. Your commitment to nurturing yourself and your baby is truly inspiring. As you move forward, remember that this book is more than just a guide; it's a companion, offering support and encouragement whenever you need it. My passion for helping new moms like yourself navigate the challenges of the fourth trimester remains unwavering, and I am honored to have shared this experience with you.

In closing, I want to leave you with an inspirational thought: with the right tools, mindset, and support, you possess the power to manage the fourth trimester with grace and ease. Embrace the changes and celebrate your victories, knowing that each step you take is a testament to you. As you continue on this path, may you find joy in the little moments and courage in the face of challenges. You are strong and capable, and motherhood is just one part of the amazing woman you are. I wish you all the best in this new chapter of your life. May it be filled with love, laughter, and endless possibilities.

REFERENCES

- *What is the fourth trimester? | Pregnancy Birth and Baby* https://www.pregnancybirthbaby.org.au/what-is-the-fourth-trimester#:~:text=The%20-fourth%20trimester%20is%20the%2012%20weeks%20following%20the%20birth,new%20life%20as%20a%20parent.
- *What To Expect While Healing After Giving Birth* https://health.clevelandclinic.org/postpartum-recovery
- *Postpartum depression: Tips for coping with it* https://www.medicalnewstoday.com/articles/320005
- *Postpartum Support International - PSI* https://www.postpartum.net/
- *Postpartum: Stages, Symptoms & Recovery Time* https://my.clevelandclinic.org/health/articles/postpartum#:~:text=The%20entire%20process%20can%20take,feel%20more%20intense%20during%20breastfeeding.
- *Cesarean section - Recovery - NHS* https://www.nhs.uk/conditions/caesarean-section/recovery/
- *Pelvic Floor Health for New Moms* https://www.voicesforpfd.org/new-mothers/pelvic-floor-health-for-new-moms/

- *9 Diastasis Recti Exercises for Postpartum Ab Separation* https://www.whattoexpect.com/first-year/your-health/diastasis-recti-exercises/
- *Postpartum depression - Symptoms and causes* https://www.mayoclinic.org/diseases-conditions/postpartum-depression/symptoms-causes/syc-20376617
- (2018). United States: Heller Helps Introduce Bill to Support Treatment for Babies Exposed to Opioids. MENA Report.
- *Coping with stress after having a baby* https://www.nhs.uk/conditions/baby/support-and-services/coping-with-stress-after-having-a-baby/
- *Talk therapy cuts risk of postpartum depression* https://www.nih.gov/news-events/nih-research-matters/talk-therapy-cuts-risk-postpartum-depression#:~:text=Overall%2C%20the%20odds%20of%20women,developing%20postpartum%20mental%20health%20conditions.
- *Postpartum anxiety mindfulness exercises - March of Dimes* https://www.marchofdimes.org/sites/default/files/2023-04/CS_MOD_ISWM_ShortForm_Mindfulness.pdf
- *Steps and Signs of a Good Latch - WIC Breastfeeding Support* https://wicbreastfeeding.fns.usda.gov/steps-and-signs-good-latch
- *Handling Infant Formula Safely: What You Need to Know* https://www.fda.gov/food/buy-store-serve-safe-food/handling-infant-formula-safely-what-you-need-know
- *Sleep Training: Definition & Techniques* https://www.sleepfoundation.org/baby-sleep/sleep-training
- *Skin-to-Skin Contact: How Kangaroo Care Benefits Your ...* https://www.healthychildren.org/English/ages-stages/baby/preemie/Pages/About-Skin-to-Skin-Care.aspx
- *Postpartum Nutrition Guide* https://www.chfs.ky.gov/agencies/dph/dmch/nsb/Documents/PostpartumNutrition.pdf

- *Meal Planning Apps for Working Moms* https://corporettemoms.com/meal-planning-apps/
- *Nourishing New Mothers: The Crucial Role of Hydration and ...* https://www.lpiphysicaltherapy.com/blog/hydration-nutrition-postpartum#:~:text=Why%20It%20Matters%3A%20Postpartum%20constipation,foods%20to%20optimize%20digestive%20health.
- *Exercise After Pregnancy* https://www.acog.org/womens-health/faqs/exercise-after-pregnancy
- *The Transition to Parenthood: Relationship Tips for New ...* https://www.gottman.com/blog/the-transition-to-parenthood-relationship-tips-for-new-parents/
- *Co-parenting: getting the balance right* https://raisingchildren.net.au/grown-ups/family-diversity/co-parenting/co-parenting
- *Sex after pregnancy: Set your own timeline* https://www.mayoclinic.org/healthy-lifestyle/labor-and-delivery/in-depth/sex-after-pregnancy/art-20045669
- *10 stressors of being a new parent and how to face them* https://www.eehealth.org/blog/2021/01/prepare-for-being-a-new-parent/
- *New baby? 7 ways to set healthy boundaries with loved ones* https://www.akronchildrens.org/inside/2023/03/29/new-baby-7-ways-to-set-healthy-boundaries-with-loved-ones/
- *Mental health in young mothers, single mothers and their ...* https://bmcpsychiatry.biomedcentral.com/articles/10.1186/s12888-019-2082-y#:~:text=Among%20mothers%20who%20were%20single,%25)%20(p%20%3D%200.005).
- *Preparing your pet for a new baby* https://www.animalhumanesociety.org/resource/preparing-your-pet-new-baby
- *What Postpartum Care Looks Like Around the World, and Why ...* https://www.healthline.com/health/pregnancy/what-post-

childbirth-care-looks-like-around-the-world-and-why-the-u-s-is-missing-the-mark#:~:text=Mexico%20has%20cuarentena%2C%20a%2030,soup)%20-called%20saam%20chil%20ill.

- *Creating a Cozy Postpartum Sanctuary at Home - Baby Boldly* https://babyboldly.com/blogs/news/creating-a-cozy-postpartum-sanctuary-at-home#:~:text=Ensure%20the%20room%20has%20good,be%20dimmed%20for%20restful%20nights.
&text=Within%20that%20designated%20space%20there,position%2C%20most%20of%20the%20day.

- *30 Useful and Quick Self-Care Apps for Moms in 2024* https://mendingtimemama.com/self-care-apps-for-moms/

- *Interventions to reduce postpartum stress in first-time mothers* https://www.ncbi.nlm.nih.gov/pmc/articles/PMC4287538/

- *Resilience and mental health among perinatal women* https://www.ncbi.nlm.nih.gov/pmc/articles/PMC11298415/

- *11 Top Tips for Returning to Work Postpartum* https://www.fdmgroup.com/news-insights/returning-to-work-postpartum/

- *Frequently Asked Questions – Pumping Breast Milk at Work* https://www.dol.gov/agencies/whd/nursing-mothers/faq

- *Juggling It All: Effective Time Management Strategies for ...* https://www.calendar.com/blog/juggling-it-all-effective-time-management-strategies-for-working-mothers/#:~:text=Prioritize%20your%20tasks.
ext=Urgent%20tasks%20should%20be%20given,or%20eliminating%20less%20important%20tasks.

- *Balancing Work and Home Life as a Mom* https://outsidethenormcounseling.com/balancing-work-and-home-life-as-a-mom/

- *Optimizing Postpartum Care* https://www.acog.org/clinical/clinical-guidance/committee-opinion/articles/2018/05/optimizing-postpartum-care

- *Bridging the postpartum gap: Best practices for training ...* https://pmc.ncbi.nlm.nih.gov/articles/PMC8328879/
- *Building a Community of Support for New Moms* https://www.womenshealth.gov/blog/community-support-new-moms
- *The effects of gratitude interventions: a systematic review ...* https://www.ncbi.nlm.nih.gov/pmc/articles/PMC10393216/

Made in the USA
Las Vegas, NV
28 March 2025

20221361R00069